Contents

Reading for Today Program Overview

The Growing Need

Illiteracy in the United States is at crisis levels. According to the National Adult Literacy Survey (NALS) over 40 million adults cannot read, write, compute, and solve problems with enough proficiency to function on the job and in society. A person needs to read at a sixth-grade level to understand a driver's license manual, an eighth-grade level to follow directions in preparing a frozen dinner, a tenth-grade level to read label instructions on a bottle of aspirin, and even higher reading levels to understand an apartment lease or an insurance policy.

Poor reading ability and/or the lack of a high school diploma make undereducated adults less able to compete in today's job market where the demand is for a literate workforce. As consumers, undereducated adults are more likely to be misled by questionable advertising, sales, and credit practices. They may even be unable to exercise one of their basic rights in a democracy—the right to vote. As parents, they may be unable to give children the help and support necessary for success in school, thus perpetuating the cycle of undereducation. Adult learners are the most rapidly-growing segment of education in the United States. Thousands are coming to adult education classes to upgrade their skills.

Reading for Today was written specifically for undereducated adult learners to satisfy their need to develop the most basic academic skill, reading. This developmental reading program takes learners from reading level 0 to reading level 6.0, the pre-GED level. The reading selections are high-interest topics of relevance to adults. The design and illustration of these books depict adults of all ages in a variety of real-life situations designed to attract and hold the learner's interest.

The first challenge facing the beginning reader is "breaking the code." But recognizing words is not enough; the reader must also understand what the words mean. To comprehend new reading material, learners must be able to make some connection with what they already know about the subject. Because adult learners have extensive experience, they bring more to the learning situation than do children. Adults often know a lot about many subjects and are able to transfer this knowledge to the written word quickly. *Reading for Today* helps adult learners build cognitive bridges from their own experience to the material they read. This increased emphasis on the building of connections is the purpose of the discussion between the instructor and learner that precedes each reading selection.

Reading for Today is the result of extensive research into how adults learn to read and what the adult learner best responds to while learning to read. Based on this research, *Reading for Today* treats reading as a holistic act in which the learner practices many subskills at the same time. As the learner progresses from unit to unit and book to book, the complex act of reading becomes easier.

An Integrated Program of Five Skill Areas

Reading for Today uses an integrated approach to teach reading skills. The new structure of the program incorporates five skill areas into each unit: sight words, phonics, comprehension, life-coping skills, and writing.

The scope and sequence is presented on pages 4–7; the skill areas are summarized below.

Sight Words Strand—Sight vocabulary is the core of words a reader recognizes instantly as a result of repeated practice. *Reading for Today* teaches the Dolch 220 List—the widely-recognized list of words that occur most frequently in printed material—as sight words. *Reading for Today* also teaches useful survival words such as *job, help, money, family,* and *plan*. Immediate recognition of common words is a skill that learners need to develop in order to become proficient readers.

Once a sight word is introduced, the learner is repeatedly exposed to that word throughout the book and in following books. Frequent practice of these words builds the learner's confidence and success in reading. Another reason why adult learners master words quickly in this program is because the vocabulary is carefully controlled, gradually introduced, and continually reviewed. Students learn new words at a steady pace and are never expected to guess at words not yet introduced.

Phonics Strand—Adults tend to learn words as a whole. With the phonics approach, learners study the individual sounds that letters represent and then blend groups of letters to form words. Learning patterns (such as consonant-vowel-consonant words) gives learners access to many other words quickly. Since breaking words into individual speech sounds and blending the sounds can be a difficult process, adult learners need to learn quickly some basic phonics techniques.

In the Introductory Book, learners study sounds in groups of four consonants and a short vowel, and are able to build words right away. Books 2–5 use known sight words and the word family approach to make the connection to phonics as soon as possible. In Book Two the learner begins with a known sight word such as *can* and builds more *–an* words through substituting the initial consonant *(ban, fan, man, pan, ran, tan)*. In this systematic way, learners master the basics of phonics and expand their vocabulary quickly.

Writing Strand—For most adult learners, the ability to write clear sentences and paragraphs is as important as the ability to read effectively. When adults answer questions on job application forms or compose brief notes to relatives, friends, children's teachers, and employers, writing is a life-coping skill.

English includes many difficult concepts such as irregular plurals, irregular verbs, contractions, and abbreviations. Adult learners need to know these concepts in order to read and write effectively. *Reading for Today* includes writing skills in every unit of Books 1–6.

Writing can also be a personal activity that allows learners to express their ideas in a personal journal. A variety of writing activities are suggested in the lesson plans in this teacher's guide. Language experience stories and journal writing are emphasized.

 From the earliest books, learners also write their own sentences on review word pages, sight word pages, and comprehension pages. These opportunities for students to produce original writing are indicated by this writing icon. Each unit in the accompanying *Reading for Today* workbooks concludes with a writing page that reinforces reading skills and helps learners master words by using the words in their own free writing.

Comprehension/Critical Thinking Strand—The comprehension strand in *Reading for Today* helps learners gain the skills they need to understand what they read. Books 1–3 focus on the basic comprehension skills: recalling facts and details, finding the main idea, ordering events and ideas in a time sequence, identifying words through context clues, predicting, and summarizing. Practice with these skills also helps to prepare learners for standardized tests.

These basic comprehension skills are reviewed and practiced in later books as learners move on to develop higher-level thinking skills such as inferring, drawing conclusions, determining cause and effect, comparing and contrasting, classifying, making judgments, and distinguishing fact and opinion. All these skills are vital on the job and at home.

Life Skills Strand—Adults who enter a reading program usually have developed numerous strategies for coping as non-readers in a print-oriented society. Adults who seek help do so for very personal reasons. While the reasons differ from person to person, adults all have one thing in common, the hope they can change their lives by learning to read. An adult who cannot read is discouraged when trying to complete a job application, fill out a green card, or scan the classified ads for a new apartment. Addressing

these short-term needs is an important step for most adult learners. They can readily appreciate the correlation between reading and writing and survival in today's complex society.

Life-coping themes are central to each story in Books 2–6. High-interest themes such as finding ways to increase income, changing careers, and working together for change motivate learners who begin the program and keep them interested in staying with it. These themes are based on adult competencies in consumer economics, job knowledge, health and safety, community resources, and government and law. Adult learners can relate to these story themes and situations because of their own life experiences. This combination stimulates discussion of "what-ifs" and helps develop problem-solving skills.

Other Features of the Program

Unit Reviews—Books 2–5 have a Unit Review that concludes every unit in the book. The Introductory Book and Book One have a combination of periodic review pages within units and end-of-unit reviews. All of these reviews provide an opportunity for both students and instructors to assess the student's progress with the skills covered in the unit.

Final Review—All seven student books contain a Final Review that covers all the skills in the book. It may be used as an informal check of a student's progress on the skills in each book or as a formal assessment of the student's mastery of the skills and readiness to move to the next level.

Learner Checklist—The Learner Checklist at the back of each student book provides a convenient way to record a student's progress on all the skills in the book.

Instructor Notes—In all seven student books, brief notes at the bottom of each page give the instructor helpful information about teaching that page.

At Your Leisure—This two-page section in Books 2–5 provides students a chance to read and enjoy other kinds of material. Each At Your Leisure section contains a poem and a prose selection written on the same topic. The poems are real pieces of literature written by well-known authors. The prose selections are the kinds of reading that adults might find in magazines and newspapers. The reading in this section is not confined to the controlled vocabulary in the rest of the book, and it is not tested by the Final Review.

Blackline Masters—On pages 127–137 of this guide is an assortment of blackline masters designed to be used with various activities in the student books. Instructors are directed to these blackline masters in the Instructor Notes on the pages where they might most appropriately be used. Instructors may also find additional ways to use them.

Related Materials

Workbooks—Books 1–6 have accompanying workbooks that provide additional, independent practice to help learners master reading skills. The workbooks contain new stories, writing pages, and exercises that review the vocabulary and skills covered in the student books. Each workbook also contains a section that provides teaching suggestions and other information for the instructor. Instructors are referred to the workbooks in the Instructor Notes in the student books.

Instructor Training Program—This training package contains an Instructor Training Manual, a video, and a set of instructor certificates. It is designed to give a hands-on experience for instructors learning to use *Reading for Today* with their adult students.

Scope and Sequence of Program Strands

Book Title	Sight Words/Vocabulary	Phonics/Word Study
Introductory Book	• Visual discrimination of letters/words • Recognition of letters of the alphabet • Sight words in context • Question words *(who, what, when, where, why)* • 157 words total	• Initial and final consonants • Short vowels and CVC word pattern • Long vowels and CVC + *e* word pattern

Book One	• Introduces 120 sight words, function words, and number words
	• Reviews 143 words from the *Introductory Book*
		• Letter-sound associations reviewed for consonants
		  Short vowels and CVC word pattern
		  Long vowels and CVC + *e* word pattern

Book Two	• Sight word pages introduce 63 new words
	• Review word pages reinforce 143 words from the Introductory Book and 120 words from Book 1
		• Short vowels taught and reviewed through these word families:
		  Short *a* in *–an, –at, –ad, –and*
		  Short *e* in *–end, –ent, –et, –ed*
		  Short *o* in *–op, –ot*
		  Short *i* in *–in, –it*
		  Short *u* in *–ut, –un*

Book Three	• Sight word pages introduce 64 new words
	• Review word pages reinforce 84 sight words from Books 1–2
		• Long vowels taught and reviewed through these word families:
		  Long *a* in *–ake, –ay*
		  Long *i* in *–ine, –ight*
		  Long *o* in *–ope, –old*
		  Long *e* in *–eed, –eat*
		  Long *u* in *–une, –ute*
		• Short vowels reviewed through these word families: *–ag, –ell, –ip, –ig, –ug*
		• Initial consonant blends and digraphs introduced: *st, sh, wh, pr, dr, str, th, cl, tr*

Writing	Comprehension/Life Skills
• Writing letters of the alphabet • Writing words and sentences • Filling out a simple form • Language experience stories • Journal writing	• Recalling facts and details • Relating a story to one's own experience
• Adding –s, –es, –ed, and –ing endings to verbs • Writing number words • Writing sentences • Language experience stories • Journal writing	• Recalling facts and details • Relating a story to one's own experience
• Writing telling, asking, and strong feeling sentences. • Adding –s, –es, –ed, and –ing to verbs • Forming contractions • Forming the past tense of irregular verbs • Capitalizing sentences and proper names • Adding 's to form singular possessive of nouns • Writing questions with question words • Writing sentences • Journal writing	• **Comprehension skills:** predicting, summarizing, recalling facts and details, finding the main idea, inferring, sequencing events, drawing conclusions, determining cause and effect • **Life skills:** managing money, moving to find work, maintaining health, using leisure time, job safety, understanding self and others, finding a satisfying job
• Compound words • Irregular plurals • Adding –er to nouns • Using commas • Irregular verbs • Dropping final e to add –ed and –ing to verbs • Using quotation marks in dialog • Writing sentences • Journal writing	• **Comprehension skills:** predicting, summarizing, recalling facts and details, finding the main idea, inferring, sequencing events, drawing conclusions, determining cause and effect • **Life skills:** finding ways to increase income, rearing children, promoting health care, handling social relationships, learning about training programs, coping with job dissatisfaction, working together for change

Book Title	Sight Words/Vocabulary	Phonics/Word Study

Book Four	• Sight word pages introduce 84 new words
	• Review word pages reinforce 84 sight words from Books 2–3
	• Life Skill pages introduce 29 new words
		• Consonant blends taught:
		    r blends: *br, cr, dr, fr, gr, pr, str, tr*
		    s blends: *sc, sk, sl, sm, sn, sp, st, sw*
		    l blends: *bl, cl, fl, gl, pl, sl*
		• Consonant digraphs taught: *ch, sh, shr, th, wh*
		• Silent letters taught: *wr, kn, gu, gh*
		• Long vowels *i* and *e* spelled *–y* taught
		• Long and short vowels reviewed through these word families: *–y, –ink, –eet, –ean, –ock, –ate, –ack, –ank, –ing, –ub, –eep, –ear*
		• Syllables defined
		• Vowel sound schwa introduced

Book Five	• Sight word pages introduce 85 new words • Review word pages reinforce 84 sight words from Books 3–4 • Life Skill pages introduce 26 new words	• Vowel digraphs taught through these word families: *–ain, –ame, –ie, –ice, –ue, –ew, –oo, –ou, –all, –aw* • Diphthongs taught through these word families: *–oil, –oy, –own, –ound* • R-controlled vowels taught through these word families: *–ark and –orn* • Consonant blends and digraphs reviewed • Syllables and schwa reviewed

Book Six	• Definition pages introduce 70 new words
	• Vocabulary pages cover the following skills:
	    Multiple meanings Suffixes
	    Word stress Analogies
	    Prefixes and Suffixes Prefixes
	    Antonyms
	• Vocabulary, word study, and life skills pages introduce new words in context
		• Dividing words into syllables using VCV, VCCV, and consonant + *le* word patterns
		• Dictionary entries
		• Prefixes and Suffixes
		• Dictionary pronunciations
		• Dictionary accent marks

Writing	Comprehension	Life Skills
• Irregular verbs • Prefixes *re–* and *un–* • Plurals with *–ies* • Suffixes *–ly, –y, –ful, –ness* • Abbreviations and titles • Days of the week and months of the year • Journal writing	• Predicting • Summarizing • Cause and effect • Inference • Stated and implied main idea • Sequence • Context • Drawing conclusions	• Writing a letter • Reading coupons • Reading a report card • Reading a prescription • Reading park rules • Coping with shyness • Reading a schedule
• Subject-verb agreement • Adding *–er* and *–est* to adjectives • Writing a friendly letter • Changing *y* to *i* to add *–es, –ed* • Forming plural possessive of nouns • Irregular verbs • Reflexive pronouns • Journal writing	• Predicting • Summarizing • Fact and opinion • Comparing and contrasting • Sequence • Inference • Making judgments • Drawing conclusions • Classifying	• Reading help wanted ads • Reading a payment schedule • Reading a map • Telephone safety • Reading a chart • Filling out a form • Reading a menu
• Using adjectives • Writing names and titles • Writing complete sentences • Recognizing fragments • Past tense of verbs • Pronouns • Recognizing run-ons • Journal writing	• Predicting • Summarizing • Recalling facts • Character traits • Main idea • Cause and effect • Inference • Sequence • Drawing conclusions • Writer's tone and purpose • Fact and opinion	• Finding library materials • Reading abbreviations • Writing a summary of qualifications • Completing a medical form • Filling out a credit application • Being a good listener • Using an index

Profile of Adult Learners

Although adult learners are not all alike, there are certain characteristics they have in common, such as being goal-oriented, competent, and motivated. These characteristics and their implications for teaching adults are discussed below.

Confidence—Adult students come to the learning situation afraid they won't be able to learn, because they have already failed once in school. They have no reason to believe that it will be different this time, though most hope they will succeed. Adults need materials designed for success.

Tip: The instructor can provide adults with materials that are designed for success.

Goals—Adult learners usually have a definite short-term goal when starting an educational program, such as filling out a job application, taking a driver's examination, helping children with homework, reading labels, or getting promoted. They often have long-term goals of getting a high-school diploma or GED or even going to college. Adult students want to see immediate results and growth.

Tip: Work together with your student to set achievable short-term goals. This keeps motivation high while working toward long-term goals.

Motivation—Although adult students have motives strong enough to enter a program, they are easily discouraged. They may sometimes exhibit a negative attitude because of past failures. They need individual attention and one-to-one instruction.

Tip: Give the adult learner individual attention and personalized lessons. Encourage the learner to value each small success.

Ego Defense—Many adults develop strategies to conceal their lack of education. These strategies often show up as excuses for non-performance.

Tip: Try to understand the situation and begin work at a comfort level that ensures success. Treat adults with the dignity and respect they deserve.

Competence and Varied Experiences—Because adults have jobs, hobbies, friends, and families, they bring a variety of past experiences and insights to their learning. They are mature, competent people who have been functioning in the adult world for years.

Tip: Incorporate the adult's experiences into the teaching situation whenever possible to enrich the learning.

Principles of Adult Learning

These principles are derived from the profile of the adult learner and are incorporated into *Reading for Today*.

Stimulate—Make learning experiences stimulating, but not too demanding. Adult learners are already threatened by school, so avoid giving them materials beyond their ability.

Meaningful—All learning materials should be vital and meaningful to an adult learner. The vocabulary must be adult-oriented.

Success—Make sure adult learners consistently experience success in learning.

Steps—Present skills to the adult learner in small, sequential steps so that they are not overwhelmed with too much information.

Goals—Organize each lesson around specific learning goals or outcomes. Tell learners what objective they will achieve with each lesson.

Apply—Give your adult learners opportunities to apply newly acquired skills as quickly as possible to real-life situations. Adults need to see the immediate value of each learning experience.

Integrate—Combine several skills and teach them concurrently to save time. Reading materials should supply information and ideas while developing new reading skills.

Progress—Provide adult learners with progress reports at frequent intervals. Recognition of progress toward goals can serve as an important stimulant to adult learning.

Independence—Materials should allow adults to make discoveries on their own with limited instructor supervision. Adults need independence and are capable of assuming responsibility for their own learning.

Experience—Capitalize on the adult's past experiences wherever possible.

Learning Styles

There are several systems for categorizing learning styles. While these systems may be confusing, they all have the same purpose: to make sense of the different ways in which people learn. Of course, no one category will describe all of a single student's characteristics. Most students, however, tend to prefer certain learning styles over others.

The two systems of categorizing learning styles presented here, learning modalities and left- or right-brain dominance, can help you in the following tasks.

- developing an awareness of each student's learning style
- developing an awareness of your own learning style and its effect on your instruction
- using instructional tools that are effective for all of your students
- helping students to recognize their own learning styles and adjust their study habits accordingly

Recognizing Learning Modalities

Some students are able to absorb information from lectures, others would prefer just to read the book, and still others learn best from experiments and demonstrations. Use the following lists of characteristics to recognize your students' learning modalities.

Visual learners
- learn by seeing or watching
- focus on descriptions when reading
- recognize words visually
- usually have clear, neat handwriting
- remember things by sight or by taking notes
- are distracted by movement
- solve problems by planning and making lists
- are usually quiet and do not enjoy talking

Auditory learners
- learn by listening
- focus on dialogue when reading and may move their lips or read out loud
- recognize words by sound
- may have difficulty with handwriting
- remember things by repeating them out loud or hearing them repeated
- are distracted by sounds
- solve problems by talking about them
- enjoy listening and talking

Kinesthetic or tactile learners
- learn by doing
- focus on action when reading
- are usually poor spellers
- have handwriting of uneven quality
- remember things that were done
- are easily distracted, since neither visual nor spoken presentations hold their attention
- solve problems with action
- gesture when speaking and do not listen well

Teaching for Learning Modalities

Once you have identified your students' modalities, consider using the following tips to adjust your teaching style to reach all your students.

Tips for Teaching Visual Learners
- Use charts, graphs, maps, pictures, and other visuals where appropriate.
- Make sure students can see your gestures and expressions when you are speaking.
- Use films, videos, and computers where appropriate.

Tips for Teaching Auditory Learners
- Conduct class discussions.
- Assign speeches and presentations.
- Allow students to tape record lectures.

Tips for Teaching Kinesthetic or Tactile Learners
- Conduct hands-on demonstrations and experiments.
- Assign posters, models, and other art projects.
- Allow students to move around the room.

Study Tips for Learning Modalities

Students will be more successful if they adjust their study habits to suit their learning modalities. Encourage students to use the following study tips.

Visual learners should

- highlight important points in their text in color
- take notes
- draw a picture of their ideas before they write
- illustrate their stories
- study in a quiet place
- read illustrated books
- memorize by visualizing information as a picture

Auditory learners should

- read out loud
- memorize by making up jingles or other mnemonics
- discuss their ideas out loud
- dictate their thoughts to a classmate

Kinesthetic or tactile learners should

- take plenty of study breaks
- move while learning, including chewing gum
- work standing up
- highlight texts with bright colors
- put up posters and other colorful decorations in their study spaces
- listen to music while studying
- skim reading assignments before they read in depth

Recognizing Left-Brain and Right-Brain Learners

Another way of categorizing learning styles that may be helpful is one based on the dominance of the left or right hemispheres of the brain. Use the following clues to recognize left- and right-brain learners.

Left-brain learners

- are comfortable with sequence
- work well within structures and systems
- break problems down into parts
- plan carefully and well
- are good at analysis

Right-brain learners

- excell at visual and spatial tasks
- act spontaneously
- recognize patterns
- see problems as a whole picture
- draw conclusions intuitively

Teaching Left-Brain and Right-Brain Learners

In order to engage both left-brain and right-brain learners, it is important to use a variety of teaching strategies. Consider the following to add variety to your lesson plans:

- Storytelling—Present new information or concepts in the form of a story.
- Journal Writing—Have students keep journals related to the subject.
- Publishing—Help students to publish their work in the school library or on the Internet.
- Performing—Have students act out the material as though it were a play or simulate the situation being discussed.
- Debating—Hold classroom debates on the issues you are covering.

Learning Disabilities

Even more than most adult students, those with learning disabilities come to school with a history of failure. For them, school is a place where their weaknesses and ignorance are exposed. Studying is difficult in the crowded, impoverished conditions in which many learning disabled adults live, and they may have no knowledge of the cultural facilities, such as libraries, which are available to them. In order to make their way in a literate world, many learning-disabled adults have developed an acute sensitivity to non-verbal communication and are likely to "hear" your attitudes and unexpressed thoughts, such as impatience. Such students require care and sensitivity.

Learning disabilities have a physical origin, and do not necessarily reflect on the student's intelligence. With your help, learning disabled students can master the skills they need to read and write. Simply being aware of the characteristics of learning disabled students will help you correctly diagnose problems and avoid misunderstandings. Your best source of teaching strategies for learning disabled adults may be the students themselves. Many students know which approaches work for them—and which do not.

Like most adults, learning disabled students learn best in an atmosphere of respect in which the student is treated as a partner in the learning process. Positive reinforcement is an essential tool for teaching learning disabled adults. Because they are accustomed to failure, these students can be easily discouraged. By emphasizing students' accomplishments and skills rather than their errors, you can help them to build confidence and motivate them to continue learning.

This section of the *Reading for Today* Instructor's Guide provides teaching strategies that can be used in any classroom to enhance learning disabled students' chances of success as well as information on adapting your classroom for learning disabled students.

Recognizing Learning Disabilities

Learning disabled students may have problems with cognition, perception, language, attention, and motor skills. Look for the following clues to recognize students with learning disorders. No one student will have all these characteristics; if a student has several of them, it may indicate that he or she has a learning disability.

General
- is good at speaking but poor at writing or vice versa
- has trouble concentrating and is easily distracted
- acts without thinking
- is very disorganized
- has trouble following directions
- does not meet deadlines or stick to schedules
- gets lost easily
- has difficulty memorizing or retaining information
- has difficulty with math
- has trouble telling left from right and up from down
- doesn't apply familiar ideas to new situations
- doesn't recognize his or her own errors
- has trouble correctly processing the sounds of language
- has trouble understanding spoken information

Reading Problems
- doesn't like to read
- fails to sound out words or sounds them out incorrectly
- has trouble learning and remembering new words
- comprehends written material poorly
- loses his or her place when reading
- makes errors in reading
- confuses letters or numbers, reverses them, or gets them in the wrong order
- has difficulty reading fine print and columns

Writing Problems
- is a poor speller
- has difficulty writing his or her own ideas
- has messy handwriting
- has continuing difficulty with sentence structure and punctuation
- has difficulty retrieving words from memory
- does not focus on a clear purpose for writing
- has difficulty spotting errors and revising

Speaking Problems
- pronounces words incorrectly
- has trouble blending sounds to form a word
- uses words incorrectly
- has difficulty retrieving words from memory
- has problems organizing his or her thoughts
- does not stick to the subject

Listening Problems
- hears language incorrectly
- does not understand and/or remember spoken information
- does not remember the order in which things were said

Teaching Learning Disabled Students

General Strategies
Teaching learning disabled students— especially adults—requires an approach different from that used with students with more traditional learning styles. The following strategies are effective for learning disabled adults:

1. Focus on important skills.

    Because learning is a slow process for learning disabled students, it is important to take care in choosing which skills to teach. If possible, the student should choose the skills he or she most wants to acquire.

2. Teach fewer skills in greater depth.

    If you try to teach too much in too short a time, the student will probably not learn any skill thoroughly. Choose a few skills and make sure the student masters them.

3. Teach actively and directly.

    Learning disabled students generally do not respond well to an approach in which they are led to discover concepts and skills. Tell students directly what to do and how to do it.

4. Relate skills to real life.

    Skills should be related to real life at all times and practiced in contexts similar to those encountered in everyday situations.

5. State instructional goals.

    At the beginning of each lesson, briefly state what is to be learned and explain why it is important.

6. Verify that students have mastered old skills before teaching new ones.

    Ask students to perform the previously-taught skill. If they cannot, reteach it. If they can perform the skill, introduce the new skill.

7. Model the skill.

    Perform the skill for learners while describing what you are doing and why. Then ask students to help you by telling you what you should do first, second, etc. When students grasp the skill, they are ready to practice.

8. Guide students' practice.

    If learning disabled students practice a skill incorrectly, it can be very difficult for them to re-learn it. Check students' work and correct errors immediately.

9. Practice with controlled materials.

    Use materials with a low level of difficulty. Exercises should be constructed so that there is only one correct answer. When students have mastered the skills involved, they may practice on more difficult materials.

10. Continue to practice and review skills.

    New skills should be practiced frequently. When they have been mastered, practice should be continued less frequently. Practice is essential for students to internalize skills.

11. Ask questions frequently.

Asking questions helps counter the tendency of learning disabled students to be passive learners and gives you information about the students' comprehension.

12. Correct errors immediately.

Provide the correct response and ask students to repeat it. If the error involves a procedure, go through the procedure with the student. Make sure the skill is performed correctly.

13. Help students to generalize skills.

Learning disabled students often have difficulty generalizing skills. After teaching a skill, discuss with students other contexts in which it can be applied. It is also important to make sure that students do not overgeneralize. When appropriate, discuss contexts in which the skill does not apply.

14. Involve multiple senses.

Engage as many of the student's senses as possible. Using sight, hearing, and touch to present the material allows students to use their strongest senses and helps students to remember the information.

Strategies for Specific Skills

• Learning new concepts

Most learning-disabled adults have poor learning skills. Perhaps the most important contribution you can make to their education is to teach them learning strategies which they can apply to any subject. Try the following strategies:

SQ3R—Teach students to approach new material using these steps: Survey, Question, Read, Recite, Review.

ERROR MONITORING—Students can take control of their own learning process when they recognize changes in the number and type of errors they make.

NOTETAKING—Teach students to take effective notes.

• Memory

Storing and retrieving information presents serious difficulties for most learning disabled adults. Helping students improve memorization skills will not only help the student learn to read but to perform other important life activities. Try the following strategies:

CATEGORIZING—Information is easier to remember if it is divided into categories.

COMPARING NEW INFORMATION WITH KNOWN INFORMATION—This is a skill that most people practice intuitively. Help students practice it until it becomes a habit.

DISTINGUISHING IMPORTANT FROM UNIMPORTANT INFORMATION—It can be overwhelming to try to remember a whole group of facts. Selecting one or two important facts can improve the student's chances of success.

IMAGING—Students may find information easier to remember if they picture it visually.

COLOR CODING—Encourage students to use highlighters to mark similar ideas with the same color.

MAPPING—Idea maps can give students a visual image to aid their memories.

MNEMONICS—Encourage students to make up their own mnemonics.

RHYMING IDEAS OR PUTTING THEM TO MUSIC—This can be a creative, enjoyable way to memorize.

VERBAL REPETITION—Repeating ideas out loud can help students commit them to memory.

• Comprehension

Comprehension is an essential skill that many learning-disabled adults lack. Teach comprehension by using the 5W+How questions *(Who? What? When? Where? Why?* and *How?)* frequently.

- Spelling

   Because spelling instruction helps students to focus on word patterns, it can also be helpful for improving reading skills. Use the Look, Cover, Write, Check procedure to teach spelling.

- Proofreading

   In order to isolate the words or sentences being checked, have students proofread backwards, looking at each word and then each sentence to make sure it is correct.

Classroom Accommodations for Learning Disabled Students

   Resources available for classroom accommodations vary from school to school. Each teacher must decide which accommodations are feasible and would be most helpful for his or her students.

- Testing

   Many learning disabled adults have difficulty coping with the pressure of timed tests. While taking such tests is an important skill that should be practiced, use as few timed tests as possible.

- Using computers

   HARDWARE AND SOFTWARE DESIGNED FOR EASY ACCESS—Students who find computers difficult to use can benefit from specially designed equipment and programs, including large-print displays and voice input.

   THE INTERNET—The World Wide Web can provide access to people, experiences, and information that might otherwise be out of students' reach.

   WORD PROCESSING—Students who have trouble writing by hand may prefer to use a word-processing program.

   SPELL CHECKING—Students who have trouble recognizing their own spelling errors can use spell-check programs.

- Using audiotape

   Tape recording lectures and textbooks can aid students who have difficulty reading, taking notes, or retaining verbal information.

- Using videotape

   Videotaping lectures and demonstrations can help students who are visually oriented and have difficulty retaining verbal information.

- Using notetakers

   Assigning a classmate to take notes can benefit students who have difficulty writing.

- Using a learning lab

   A learning lab is an ideal environment for providing learning disabled students with additional instruction and practice. Make sure students target only one skill on each visit to avoid becoming confused or frustrated.

Resources for Adult Learning

Adult Education Teacher's Annotated Webliography
http://www2.wgbh.org/MBCWEIS/LTC/ALRI/webliography.html

Adult Literacy Resource Institute
http://www2.wgbh.org/MBCWEIS/LTC/ALRI/alri.html

Ask ERIC
http://ericir.syr.edu

Barbara Bush Foundation for Family Literacy
http://www.barbarabushfoundation.com

Center for the Study and Treatment of Dyslexia, Middle Tennessee State University
http://www.mtsu.edu/~dyslexia/index.html

CNN's Interactive Learning Resources for Teaching
http://literacynet.org/cnnsf/

Exemplary World Wide Web Education Sites
http://www.ncsa.uiuc.edu/edu/cybered/cybered_hotlist.html

Family Education, Adult Literacy and English as a Second Language
http://www.itouch.net/~klearn/familyed.html

International Dyslexia Association
http://www.interdys.org

International Literacy Institute
http://ili2.literacy.upenn.edu/ILI

International Reading Association
http://www.reading.org

Internet Directory of Literacy and Adult Education Resources
http://novel.nifl.gov/litdir/index.html

Learning Disabilities Association of America (LDA)
http://www.ldanatl.org

Lifelong Learning Online
http://www.otan.dni.us/cdlp/lllo/home.html

Literacy Assistance Center
http://www.lacnyc.org

Literacy List
http://www2.wgbh.org.MBCWEIS/LTC/ALRI/literacylist.html

Literacy Online (NCAL)
http://literacyonline.org

National Adult Literacy and Learning Disability Center
http://www.novel.nifl.gov/naldtop.htm

National Center for Family Literacy
http://www.vmarketing.com/famlit.org

National Center for Research in Vocational Education
http://www.labor.state.ny.us

National Center for the Study of Adult Learning and Literacy (NCSALL)
http://gseweb.harvard.edu/~ncsall

National Center on Adult Literacy (NCAL)
http://litserver.literacy.upenn.edu

National Institute for Literacy (NIFL)
http://novel.nifl.gov

NIFL Regional LINCS Web Sites (links to literacy organizations in all 50 US states and the territories)
http://www.nifl.gov/hubsmap.htm

Office of Vocational & Adult Education
http://www.ed.gov/offices/OVAE

PBS Adult Learning Service
http://www.pbs.org/adultlearning

PBS LiteracyLink
http://www.pbs.org/literacy

SCANS/2000 (Johns Hopkins University Institute for Policy Studies)
http://infinia.wpmc.jhu.edu

T.H.E. Journal: Roadmap to the Web for Educators II
http://www.thejournal.com/roadmap97/roadmap2.asp

Teaching & Learning with Internet-based Resources
http://www.nifl.gov/susanc/inthome.htm

Writing: Language Experience and Journals

The connection between reading and writing is well established; good reading skills and good writing skills go hand-in-hand. Therefore, to strengthen this connection from the start, *Reading for Today* incorporates writing through language experience activities and the personal journal. Both techniques encourage learners to discover their own distinctive ways of speaking and writing. Both allow learners to create some of the material from which they learn to read.

Language Experience Activity

The Language Experience Approach, a well-known and successful technique to reading and writing instruction, is central to *Reading for Today*. In this approach, the learner's own thoughts, experiences, and words are used as a basis for instruction. A typical lesson follows these steps.

Lesson Steps:

1. The learner dictates to the instructor a story about a topic of interest to the learner.
2. The instructor writes or records the learner's words exactly as spoken.
3. The instructor reads the story back to the learner to confirm the wording.
4. The learner and the instructor read the story together. They may decide to select three to five words for intensive vocabulary practice. The instructor writes the words on index cards for the learner to practice as sight words.
5. The instructor may also point out some words in the story to reinforce a phonics lesson in *Reading for Today*. For example, the instructor can choose one or two words such as *make* or *did* from which to teach a vowel lesson based on word families.
6. The instructor asks the learner a question that adds to the story, such as, "What do you think might happen next?"
7. To review the story, the learner reads the story again and reviews the vocabulary words.
8. As the number increases, the instructor keeps a portfolio of the learner's work.

There are several benefits of including the Language Experience Approach in *Reading for Today*:

- It emphasizes the communication process.
- The learner clearly sees the relationship between spoken and written language.
- The material relates directly to the learner's unique needs, goals, and experience; therefore, it is inherently interesting to the learner.
- The learner feels pride and mastery in using his or her own words as a lesson springboard.

Journal Writing

The journal is useful for both skill-related writing and personal writing. Learners can practice the following skills in their journals:

- compiling vocabulary lists;
- practicing sight words and phonics words;
- reading and writing the new words in phrases;
- writing original sentences and paragraphs;
- recording stories, personal observations, and comments.

Because learners are often unsure of the "rules" for journal writing, read to them the following guidelines.

To the Learner: Tips for Journal Writing

- Your journal is a place to express your feelings, opinions, thoughts, likes, and dislikes. It can also be a place to collect and keep your work in one place.
- Focus on expressing your personal thoughts. Don't worry about misspellings.
- Use your journal as you read: (1) Ask yourself questions and make notes to help you make sense of what you are reading. These notes often lead to a better understanding of what you are reading. (2) As you start to read a story, predict what you think will happen. Change the prediction as you read further and have more facts. Good readers have this kind of self-talk. (3) Talk to the characters as you begin to know them. Give them advice; share how you would act in a similar situation. Approve or disapprove of their actions.

Placing Learners in the Program

Deciding which book is appropriate for an adult learner entering a reading program for the first time is important to the learner's success. Starting an adult in a book that is too difficult can cause the learner to become discouraged. To build success and confidence, place the learner in the book you are sure he or she can read with ease at the independent reading level (99% word recognition accuracy and 90% comprehension).

Alternate Methods

Five methods for initial placement of your adult learner are listed below for your convenience. Choose the method that best fits your needs.

Standardized Tests—Use all information available about the learner's reading level such as standardized test scores on the Test of Adult Basic Education or the Adult Basic Learning Examination.

Informal Reading Inventory—Administer an informal reading inventory such as the Slosson Oral Reading Test on an individualized basis. Match the learner's reading level to the appropriate *Reading for Today* book.

Reading for Today	Reading Level
Introductory Book	0–.5
Book One	.5–1.0
Book Two	1.0–2.0
Book Three	2.0–3.0
Book Four	3.0–4.0
Book Five	4.0–5.0
Book Six	5.0–6.0

Or, you can create your own informal reading inventory by selecting sample paragraphs from stories in *Reading for Today* and then placing students in the highest level book they can read comfortably.

The Alphabet and Key Words—Ask the learner to read the alphabet and a list of the key words for alphabet letters from the Introductory Book. If the learner experiences any difficulty, the Introductory Book is the appropriate place to begin instruction.

Learner Placement Form—Administer individually the Learner Placement Form located on the inside back covers of Books 1–6 and on page 139 of this guide. Make two photocopies, one for you to mark and one for the learner to read. Ask the learner to read the Book One list. If the learner knows these words or only misses one or two, proceed to the next list. If a learner misses three consecutive words, place him or her in that book.

Unit Review Pages—You may prefer to have the learner read sentences rather than word lists, or to use a combination of the two. If so, photocopy and administer the unit reviews from Books 2–6. The unit reviews practice in context the vocabulary words from each unit in that book.

Evaluating the Adult Learner

Formal and informal evaluation can be an on-going activity of both the instructor and the adult learner. Encourage learners to do periodic self-evaluations of their progress by reviewing their journals and portfolios. Below are further suggestions for evaluating the adult learner.

Book Pages—Informally check the learner's progress by reviewing his or her work. In Books 2–6, have the learner read the Back to the Story section, which applies all the skills covered in the unit.

Final Mastery—For a more formal assessment of learners' skill mastery in Books 2–6, photocopy and administer the Unit Review after the learner completes each unit. Then as a final check on whether the learner has retained mastery of these skills, administer the Final Review.

Conferences—Meet with learners periodically to discuss their progress. Ask them for a self-evaluation. Then review some pages in the book and their journals. Ask learners to keep a list in their journals of words they need to practice further. Then agree on a plan for achieving mastery.

Introductory Book

Overview

The Introductory Book is an entry-level literacy text designed for adults with no prior reading or writing skills. It spans the 0–.5 reading level and introduces the alphabet and 157 new words. The book also provides a comprehensive presentation of letter-sound associations and simple language skills common to beginning reading instruction. In addition, this book introduces and reinforces the reading-writing connection through the frequent use of language experience stories and personal journals.

Lesson plans for teaching the three units of the Introductory Book begin on page 19 of this guide. Each lesson plan is a model for teaching all similar student pages; for example, there is one model lesson for all the initial letter pages, and page numbers for those corresponding pages are listed just below the lesson title.

Unit 1 teaches the visual recognition of the letters of the alphabet in capital and small letter form using key words and pictures. Each page introduces two letters of the alphabet with handwriting models, a key picture, and a key word for each letter. Each section consists of six letters and ends with a review page. A handwriting chart of the capital and small letters provides models for the student and helps the instructor check informally which letters and numbers the student already knows. A library card application form provides practice for students in writing their names, addresses, and other basic information. All units conclude with a review that may be used as a mastery test.

Unit 2 teaches letter-sound associations for consonants and short vowels which quickly enable students to read words. Consonants are presented in the initial and final positions, and short vowels are taught in the initial and medial positions. Each page introduces one sound with its key picture and word. After studying four consonants and a vowel, the student can blend sounds to read simple words in the consonant-short vowel-consonant (CVC) spelling pattern.

Then students use those known words as a springboard from which to write a language experience story. Reading and writing their own ideas make learning to read relevant and personalized.

After students have mastered eight consonants and two vowels, they can read the first Read a Story page. Vocabulary in all the stories is carefully controlled to ensure success and to avoid the frustration of encountering unknown words. Any necessary sight words are identified for the instructor to review with the student. The Think About It activity that follows the story asks *who, what, when, where, why,* and *how* questions that determine the student's comprehension of the story. The student can discuss the answers with the instructor.

The Read and Write page is a language experience activity designed to reinforce the connection between reading and writing. This page lists familiar words for students to use to write stories from their own experiences. Students dictate the story to the instructor who writes it in the book. Then students copy it in their journals, make up a title for it, and practice reading the story to the instructor.

Unit 3 presents long vowel sounds using key words that follow the consonant-vowel-consonant + silent e (CVC + *e*) spelling pattern. Each page introduces one vowel, and each lesson contrasts long and short vowel sounds in CVC words and CVC + *e* words. The unit continues the use of language experience activities. Just before the last unit review, students read a longer story resembling the stories in upper-level books.

Final Review. A Final Review assesses the student's mastery of consonants in the initial and final positions, short vowels in CVC words, and long vowels in CVC + *e* words.

Word List. A master Word List of all the words introduced in this book is on the inside back cover of the student book.

UNIT 1, LESSON 1

Letters of the Alphabet
Pages 1–2, 3–5, 7–9, 11–13, 15–18

I. LESSON OVERVIEW

This lesson introduces the capital and small letters of the alphabet and is a model for teaching all the letters of the alphabet. As an introduction, have students read the signs on pages 1–2.

II. STUDENT OUTCOMES

The student will recognize, identify, and write the capital and small letters of the alphabet.

III. PROCEDURES

Adapt the procedures in this lesson for page 3 to present all the letters of the alphabet.
Exercise 1.   Write the letters *Aa, Bb.* Pronounce the letters as the student listens, and have the student repeat them. Ask the student to identify the key pictures *apple* and *bed.* Say that *apple* begins with *a* and *bed* begins with *b.* Point out the difference between capital (upper-case) and small (lower-case) letters. Have the student write the capital and small letters for *Aa* and *Bb* on the lines provided.
Exercise 2.   Have the student circle *A* and *a.*
Exercise 3.   Have the student circle *B* and *b.*

IV. FOLLOW-UP ACTIVITIES

The following activities are designed to reinforce the student's visual recognition of the letters of the alphabet.
• Ask the student to make flash cards for each letter of the alphabet. Have the student write the capital and small letter on one side and the key picture name on the other. If a student confuses the small *b* and *d,* have him or her write the letter *c.* Then have the student draw a vertical line next to the letter *c* to transform it into the letter *d.* Have the student keep the flash cards in alphabetical order.
• Write these animal names: *ant, bird, bat,* and *antelope.* Ask the student to circle the first letter in each animal name as he or she names the letter.

• Ask the student to bring a newspaper. Have the student find words that begin with *Aa* and *Bb,* circle the words, and underline the first letter. Read the words to the student.
• Have the student think of items at home that begin with *a* and *b.* Have the student dictate the words to you: *barbecue grill, apple, bottle, ashtray,* and *book.* Write the words and read them back to the student. Have the student copy the words.

UNIT 1, LESSON 2

Review: Letters of the Alphabet
Pages 6, 10, 14, 19

I. LESSON OVERVIEW

This lesson reviews the capital and small letters of the alphabet and is a model for reviewing all the letters of the alphabet.

II. STUDENT OUTCOMES

The student will recognize, identify, and write the capital and small letters of the alphabet.

III. PROCEDURES

Adapt the procedures in this lesson for page 6 to review all the letters of the alphabet.
Exercise 1.   Have the student trace the capital and small letters *Aa, Bb, Cc, Dd, Ee,* and *Ff.*
Exercise 2.   Have the student write the letters from Exercise 1 on the lines provided.
Exercise 3.   Have the student write the missing capital and small letters.
Exercise 4.   Have the student match the capital and small letters.
Exercise 5.   Have the student circle the letters in the words to the right that correspond to each review letter.

IV. FOLLOW-UP ACTIVITIES

The following activities are designed to reinforce the student's visual recognition of the letters of the alphabet.
• Ask students to get their alphabet flash cards. Choose several letters at random and ask students

to identify them. Then have students arrange them in sequential order. Ask students to find the flash cards that come immediately before and after each letter and place them there. Ask students to say the letters aloud.

• Have the student bring a magazine. Ask the student to look for words beginning with capital and small letters *Aa, Bb, Cc, Dd, Ee,* and *Ff.* Have the student dictate the words to you. Write the words and read them back to the student. Have the student copy the words.

• Ask the student to look around the room and identify objects that begin with *Aa, Bb, Cc, Dd, Ee,* and *Ff: clock, desk, basket* for trash, *frame* for a picture, *armrest.* Write the words. Read the words and ask the student to repeat them. Have the student copy the words.

• Ask the student to select four or five words from the activity above. Have the student make flash cards of these words and add them to the deck of cards in alphabetical order behind the letters the words begin with.

UNIT 1, LESSON 3

Final Review: Aa–Zz
Pages 20–21

I.   LESSON OVERVIEW

This lesson reviews and assesses the student's visual recognition and identification of the capital and small letters of the alphabet. Use this lesson as a review or as a test.

II.   STUDENT OUTCOMES

The student will recognize and identify the capital and small letters of the alphabet.

III.   PROCEDURES

Page 20, Exercise 1. Have the student identify the capital letters and supply the letters that are missing: *B, C, E, F, H, J, L, O, Q, R, T, V, X,* and *Y.*

Exercise 2. Have the student match the capital and small letters by drawing a line connecting them.

Page 21, Exercise 1. Have the student identify the small letters and write the missing letters: *c, e, f, h, j, k, m, p, q, s, u, w,* and *z.*

Exercise 2. Have the student circle the letters in the words to the right that correspond to each review letter.

Page 22–23, The Alphabet. Have students use these pages as a reference when writing the upper- and lower-case letters of the alphabet in printing, or manuscript, style and in handwriting style.

Page 24, Numbers. Have students use this page to practice writing numbers.

Page 25, Write. Have students complete the form, using what they have learned about writing the alphabet and numbers.

IV.   FOLLOW-UP ACTIVITIES

The following activities are designed to reinforce the student's visual recognition of the letters of the alphabet.

• If a student does poorly on the final review exercises, ask him or her to identify the key pictures for each letter and match the flash card of the letter with the key picture.

• Using flash cards, show the student letters at random. Have the student identify the letter and dictate a word beginning with that letter. Write the words. Ask the student to make flash cards for several of the words dictated.

• Ask the student to complete the following crossword puzzle.

UNIT 2, LESSON 1

Initial Consonants
Pages 26–29, 36–39, 47–50, 58–61, 68–71

I. LESSON OVERVIEW

This lesson presents the initial consonant sounds and is a model for teaching all initial consonants.

II. STUDENT OUTCOMES

The student will recognize and identify the initial consonants, and read and write words with initial consonants.

III. PROCEDURES

Adapt the procedures in this lesson for page 26 to present all the initial consonants.

Exercise A. Write the capital (upper-case) *M* and small (lower-case) *m* and the key word *money*. Have the student identify the key picture on page 26 as money. Read the key sentence, "Money begins with the m sound," while the student follows along. Read and write other words that begin with *m* such as *moon, me, month,* and *mirror.* (For more example words, see the Word List on the inside back cover.) Ask the student to suggest additional words that begin with *m*. Write them. Say the words and have the student repeat them emphasizing the m sound. Have the student write the capital and small *m* several times in the space provided.

Exercise B. Have the student identify the pictures: *man, mat, mop, bed, table, milk, map,* and *mail.* Have the student listen for the initial sound in each word. Ask the student to write *m* under the pictures that begin with the *m* sound. If the picture name does not start with *m*, the student should leave the space blank.

Exercise C. Ask the student to choose a word that begins with *m*. Have the student dictate a sentence to you using the *m* word. Write the sentence and read it back to the student.

Journal. You may want the student to copy the sentence in a journal and circle the words beginning with the *m* sound. Encourage each student to start a journal. It can be divided into sections for vocabulary, sample sentences, and creative writing. Writing in the journal should be an ongoing activity for the student.

Exercise D. Have the student reread the sentence from Exercise C and circle the words with *M* and *m*. Then have the student write the *m* words.

IV. FOLLOW-UP ACTIVITIES

The following activities are designed to reinforce the student's understanding of all the initial consonant sounds.

• Ask the student to choose four or more words that begin with m such as *money, milk, man,* and *make.* Have the student make flash cards of these words and read them aloud. Review the words from time to time and add more words to the deck.

• Ask students to visualize a room and to think of an object in the room that begins with the letter *m*. For example, if the visualized room is a bedroom, students might think of a mattress; if the room is a kitchen, students might think of a microwave oven. Write the name of the room and list the word or words under the appropriate heading. Read the words back. Have students copy them in their journals and circle the initial letter *m* in each word.

• Have the student bring a department or specialty store catalog. Ask the student to draw circles around the objects beginning with the letter *m* (a washing machine, a mop, a mixer, a magazine rack).

• Help students plan a meal using foods beginning with the letter *m*. Ask the students to suggest items such as mustard greens, milk, mayonnaise, meat, muffins, macaroni, marshmallows, manicotti, and melon. Write the words for students to copy. Have students dictate a sentence to you using some of the menu words: "Mike had milk, macaroni, meat, and muffins for lunch." Have students copy the sentence in their journals.

• Ask students to look out a window for objects beginning with *m*. Write the words. Ask students to make up a sentence using one or more of the *m* words. Write the sentence and read it back to students. Have students copy the sentence in their journals and circle the initial *m*.

UNIT 2, LESSON 2

Initial Short Vowels
Pages 31, 41, 52, 62, 74

I. LESSON OVERVIEW

This lesson introduces the initial short vowels and is a model for teaching all initial short vowels.

II. STUDENT OUTCOMES

The student will recognize and identify the initial short vowels, and read and write words with initial short vowels.

III. PROCEDURES

Adapt the procedures in this lesson for page 31 to present all the initial short vowels.

Exercise A. Write the capital and small *a* and identify the key word *apple*. Read the key sentence, "Apple begins with the short *a* sound." Write other words that begin with short *a* such as *actor, ask, at,* and *after*. (For more example words, see the Word List on the inside back cover.) Ask the student to suggest additional words that begin with short *a*. Write them. Say the words and have the student repeat them emphasizing the short *a* sound. Have the student write the capital and small *a* several times in the space provided.

Exercise B. Have the student identify the pictures: *animals, ant, ax, key, dishes, astronaut, alligator,* and *apple*. Have the student listen for the initial sound in each word and write *a* under the pictures that begin with the short *a* sound.

Exercise C. Ask the student to choose a word that begins with short *a*. Have the student dictate

a sentence to you using the short *a* word. Write the sentence and read it back to the student.

Exercise D. Have the student circle the words beginning with short *a* in the sentence from Exercise C. Then have students write the short *a* words. Have students copy the sentence in their journals.

IV. FOLLOW-UP ACTIVITIES

The following activities are designed to reinforce the student's understanding of all the initial short vowel sounds.

• Ask students to bring magazines. Ask them to search for objects beginning with the short *a* sound. Have students circle the pictures and dictate the names to you. Ask students to say the words with you. Then have students copy the words in their journals and circle the letter *a*.

• Bring in a map of your state. Divide the map into sections. Ask the student to explore different sections of the map for towns or cities whose names begin with short *a*. Have the student copy the names of towns and circle the short *a*.

• Ask the student to bring something he or she wants to read. Have the student scan for words that begin with short *a*. Read the sentence containing the short *a* word to the student. Ask the student to read it back to you. Then have the student copy the sentence and circle the short *a* words.

UNIT 2, LESSON 3

Medial Short Vowels
Pages 32, 42, 53, 63, 75

I. LESSON OVERVIEW

This lesson introduces the short vowel sounds in words having the consonant-short vowel-consonant (CVC) spelling pattern. Use it as a model for teaching all the short vowels in the medial position.

II. STUDENT OUTCOMES

The student will recognize and identify the short vowels in the medial position in consonant-short vowel-consonant (CVC) words, and read and write words with the medial short vowels.

III. PROCEDURES

Adapt the procedures in this lesson for page 32 to present all the medial short vowels.

Exercise A. Have the student identify the key picture *man*. Read the key sentence, "Man has the short *a* sound." Read and write other words with the medial short *a* such as *mat, van, pan, bag,* and *cab.* (For more example words, see the Word List on the inside back cover.) Ask the student to suggest additional words that contain the medial short *a*. Write them. Point out that when words have the CVC spelling pattern, the vowel sound is usually short. Say the words and have the student repeat them emphasizing the short *a* sound. Have the student write *a* several times in the space provided.

Exercise B. Have the student identify the pictures: *gas, fan, can, olive, ham, cat, egg,* and *van.* Have the student listen for the medial short *a* sound in each word and write *a* under the pictures that have the short *a* sound.

Exercise C. Ask the student to dictate a sentence to you using at least one medial short *a* word. Write the sentence and read it back to the student.

Exercise D. Have the student circle the words with the medial short *a* in the sentence from Exercise C. Then have students write the words. Have students copy the sentence in their journals.

IV. FOLLOW-UP ACTIVITIES

The following activities are designed to reinforce the student's understanding of all the medial short vowel sounds.

• Introduce the student to four word families: *–am, –ab, –ad,* and *–ag.* Write the family names. Have the student add initial consonants to the family names to spell words: *d–am, h–am, j–ab, c–ab, p–ad, b–ag, l–ag.* Point out

the consonant-short vowel-consonant (CVC) spelling pattern. Ask the student to dictate more CVC words for each family. Write each word under the appropriate family group. Have the student make flash cards of these words and read them aloud.

• Ask the student to listen as you read the following words from the *–ag* word family: *bag, rag, tag,* and *wag.* Ask the student what the words have in common. Help the student conclude that all the words have the medial short *a* sound and all the words sound alike (rhyme). Now read another list of words: *bad, dad, dog.* Ask the student what is different about this group. Help the student conclude that dog does not sound like the other words because it has a different vowel sound.

UNIT 2, LESSON 4

Review: Consonants and Vowels in Context

Pages 33–34, 43–44, 54–55, 64–65, 76–77

I. LESSON OVERVIEW

This lesson reviews four consonants and one short vowel and is a model for reviewing all consonants and vowels in context.

II. STUDENT OUTCOMES

The student will recognize and identify consonants in the initial position and the short vowels in the initial and medial positions.

III. PROCEDURES

Adapt the procedures in this lesson for page 33 to present all the Review pages.

Write *m, d, f, g,* and *a.* Review the key word for each letter and ask the student to give more examples.

"*Money* begins with the *m* sound."
"*Dog* begins with the *d* sound."
"*Food* begins with the *f* sound."
"*Go* begins with the *g* sound."
"*Apple* begins with the short *a* sound."
"*Man* has the short *a* sound."

Page 33, Exercise A. Have the student identify the pictures: *man, football, darts, go, feather, ax, game,* and *money.* Then have him or her identify the letter that stands for the first sound in each word and write the letter under the picture.
Exercise B. Have the student identify each picture *(map, fan, and cat)* and circle the word that names the picture. Then have him or her write the word under the picture.
Page 34. Have the student identify the pictures: *mop, leaf, ham, dam, fan, bed, mat, ax, dog, map, gas,* and *desk.* Have the student write the letter that completes each word.

IV. FOLLOW-UP ACTIVITIES

The following activities are designed to review and reinforce the student's understanding of letter-sound associations for consonants and short vowels.
• To review letter-sound associations for *m, d, f,* and *g,* dictate the word pairs: *man* and *ham, dog* and *bed, follow* and *roof,* and *good* and *flag.* Have the student write the letter for the initial sound of the first word in the pair and the final sound for the second *(m–an, ha–m).*
To review the letter-sound associations for the short *a,* dictate the words *am, map, bag, dad, apple,* and *act.* Have the student circle the short *a* in each word and identify its position as either initial or medial.
• Have the student bring a menu from a take-out restaurant. Write the letters *m, d, f, g,* and *a.* Read from the menu. Have the student identify foods that begin or end with the *m, d, f, g,* or *a* sounds. Some examples include: *fudge* cake, *gumbo, beef, fettuccine,* ranch *dressing, meat* sauce, *appetizers,* and *apple pie.*
• Have the student make a shopping list of items beginning or ending with *m, d, f, g,* or *a* that can be purchased in a large discount store. Write the student's suggestions under the appropriate letter. Some items on the list might be: *motor oil, filter, dog food, antifreeze, broom, mop, batteries, games, fan, dress,* and *ax.*

UNIT 2, LESSON 5
Final Consonants
Pages 30, 40, 51, 73

I. LESSON OVERVIEW
This lesson introduces the final consonant sounds and is a model for teaching all final consonants.

II. STUDENT OUTCOMES
The student will recognize and identify the final consonants, and read and write words with final consonants.

III. PROCEDURES
Adapt the procedures in this lesson for page 30 to present all the final consonants.
Exercise A. To review letter-sound associations for *m, d, f,* and *g,* ask the student to recall the key words *money, dog, food,* and *go.* Ask the student to listen for the sound that begins each key word. Then have the student write the letter that stands for the first sound of each key word as you reread the words.
Help the student to identify the key pictures: *ham, bed, leaf,* and *log.* Tell the student that the letter *m* stands for the same sound whether it comes at the beginning, the end, or in the middle of a word: *man, ham, lemon.* Then have the student identify the pictures: *jam, bread, dam, game, gas, goat, guitar, desk.* Have the student circle the letter that stands for the last sound of the word.
Exercise B. For items 1–4, dictate a pair of words and have the student write the letter that stands for the last sound: *ham* and *gum, dog* and *flag, lid* and *bed, leaf* and *roof.*
For items 5–8, say the words *dam, leaf, dog,* and *mad.* Have the student listen for the last sound in each word and write it.

IV. FOLLOW-UP ACTIVITIES
The following activities are designed to reinforce the student's understanding of all the final consonant sounds.

• Write *m, d, f,* and *g.* Ask the student to suggest words that end with these consonants such as *am, team, pad, good, chief, stuff, bag,* and *wig.* (For more example words, see the Word List on the inside back cover). Write the words under the correct letter. Then have the student make flash cards with the letter that stands for the final sound on one side and a word that ends in that sound on the other. Have the student circle the letter that stands for the final sound in each word (for example: *team* or *game*).

• Ask students to think of first names that end in *m, d, f,* or *g* such as *Kim, Fred, Cliff,* and *Meg.* Then ask students to suggest last names that end in *m, d, f,* or *g: Putnam, Ford, McDuff,* and *Goldberg.* Have students copy the names in their journals for use in creative writing exercises.

• Ask students to bring in several newspapers. Have students search the headlines for words ending in *m, d, f,* or *g* and circle the final letter. Have students add these words to their journals.

• Ask students to choose several words from those in the activities above and create a simple sentence. For example, *Meg, wig,* and *bag* may be combined with other words to form the sentence, "Meg keeps her wig in a plastic bag." Write the sentence and ask students to record it in their journals.

UNIT 2, LESSON 6

Read and Write
(Language Experience Activity)
Pages 35, 46, 57, 67, 79

I. LESSON OVERVIEW

This lesson introduces the Read and Write page, which is a language experience activity (LEA). Use this lesson as a model for teaching all the Read and Write pages in Unit Two.

II. STUDENT OUTCOMES

Student will apply their knowledge of letter-sound associations for consonants and short vowels to create a story.

III. PROCEDURES

Adapt the procedures in this lesson for page 35 to present all the Read and Write pages.
The language experience activity lets students use their own experience and words to create a story.

Exercise A. Read the words: *dog, money, food, go, ham, bed, leaf, log, apple,* and *man.* Ask the student to suggest relationships among the words such as *dog* and *food* or *leaf* and *apple.*

Exercise B. Have the student copy the words. Ask the student to choose the words that he or she can connect in a story.

Exercise C. (Language Experience Activity) Have the student tell a story or describe an experience using one or more of the words from Exercise B. Write the story exactly as the student tells it. Read the story back to the student. Have the student copy the story in the journal and practice reading it to you. For example, a student could make up a story such as the one below using the words *man, dog, food, apple,* and *ham.*

A man saw that his dog had no food, so he walked to the grocery store to buy some. At the store the man saw a big apple that he thought would taste good with some leftover ham he had. He bought the apple and went home. When he saw his dog, the man realized he had forgotten to get dog food. He turned around and went back to the store.

Exercise D. Help the student create a title for the story by asking questions that provide clues about the story's main idea. For example, "What words can we use in a title to tell something about what happens?" Write the title that the student creates and have him or her copy it above the story.

IV. FOLLOW-UP ACTIVITIES

The following activities are designed to reinforce the student's understanding of letter-sound associations for consonants and short vowels in the context of words in the story.

• Read the words *boat, summer, bee, hat, work, watermelon, lake,* and *tire.* Ask students to copy the words and choose the ones they will use to tell you a story. Have students dictate the story to you. Write the story and read it back to students. Have students copy the story in their journals and practice reading it to you. Have students make up a title by asking Who?, What?, and Why? questions about the story. Have them write the title above the story.

• Have students bring in a story for you to read aloud. Discuss the story with students and help them pick out clues about the story's main idea by asking questions beginning with *What* and *Why.* Have students write the questions and possible answers in their journals as models for analyzing future stories.

UNIT 2, LESSON 7

Read a Story (Comprehension)
Pages 45, 56, 66, 78

I.   LESSON OVERVIEW

This lesson introduces a story, frequently used sight words, and *who* and *what.* Use it as a model for teaching all Read a Story pages.

II.   STUDENT OUTCOMES

The student will recognize sight words, read and write words that create a story, and recall facts and details of the story.

III.   PROCEDURES

Adapt the procedures in this lesson for page 45 to present all the Read a Story pages.
Introduce the sight words: *the, to, a, and, by, is, that, asked, said, from* and *about.* Tell the student that he or she must learn to recognize sight words by memorizing through repeated practice. Point out that the *–ed* on *asked* indicates action that occurred in the past.
Read.   Read each sentence and the word choices to the student. Ask the student to circle the word that best completes each sentence and

write it in the blank. Have the student practice reading the story to you.
Think About It.   Introduce the words *who* and *what* as sight words. Then read the questions and discuss the answers together. Remind students that a story's title provides a clue about the main idea of the story. Ask students to suggest a title for the story. Write it. Have students copy the title and the story in their journals.

IV.   FOLLOW-UP ACTIVITIES

The following activities are designed to reinforce students' recognition of sight words and their comprehension of a story.
• Have students make flash cards for the sight words: *the, to, a, and, by, is, that, asked, said, from,* and *about.* Have students write the sight words in their journals and practice reading them.
• Have the student bring in a story. Read the story to the student and discuss it together. Help the student frame questions about the story using *what* and *who* and answer the questions. Ask the student to explain the title's connection to the story. Let the student practice reading the story. Help the student as necessary.

UNIT 2, LESSON 8

End of Unit Review
Pages 80–81

I.   LESSON OVERVIEW

The lesson reviews and assesses the student's grasp of the letter-sound associations for consonants and short vowels. Use this lesson as a review or as a test.

II.   STUDENT OUTCOMES

The student will recognize all consonants and short vowels, and read and write words with initial and final consonants and initial and medial short vowels.

III. PROCEDURES

Ask the student to identify the pictures on page 80: *fan, dam, zip code, cat, quilt, box, gas, vet, man, ham, dog,* and *six.* Have the student identify the pictures on page 81: *bat, jet, cup, ax, web, jam, yell, can, bed, zoo, king,* and *rug.* Have the student say each picture name and write the letter that completes each word and then read the words to you. Check the student's work.

IV. FOLLOW-UP ACTIVITIES

The following activities are designed to reteach and enrich the student's understanding of letter-sound associations for consonants and short vowels.

• If the student cannot recognize and identify some of the consonants and short vowel sounds, ask him or her to use the flash cards to review the sounds. Have the student identify the key picture name for each consonant and short vowel. If the student is unsure of short vowel sounds, review the word families. Remind the student that words in a word family have the same medial vowel sound and final consonant sound.

• Ask the student to answer the following riddles. Have him or her say the words that the clues suggest.

1. It begins like *cat* and rhymes with *pup.* (cup)
2. It begins like *hot* and rhymes with *bat.* (hat)
3. It begins like *ran* and rhymes with *bug.* (rug)
4. It begins like *zebra* and rhymes with *cone.* (zone)
5. It begins like *bus* and rhymes with *ox.* (box)
6. It begins like *yarn* and rhymes with *bell.* (yell)
7. It begins like *pot* and rhymes with *man.* (pan)
8. It begins like *quit* and rhymes with *sick.* (quick)

9. It begins like *van* and rhymes with *best.* (vest)
10. It begins like *rag* and rhymes with *zip.* (rip)

• Write a blank line followed by a vowel and consonant. Use these word families: *–ad, –an, –in, –eg,* and *–un.* Have the student draw a card from a deck of consonant flash cards and write the letter in the blank before each vowel-consonant combination. Ask the student to decide if the letters form a real word. For example, if the student draws an *l,* the combinations are *lad, lan, lin, leg,* and *lun.* Only *lad* and *leg* are real words. Then ask the student to choose another consonant. Substituting *p* for *l* produces *pad, pan, pin, peg,* and *pun*–all real words.

• Have the student find as many words as possible in the word search below. The words may be written forward, backward, or up and down. Some words overlap. The puzzle contains the following words: *add, and, ant, ax, bad, bet, dab, big, boy, dip, dog, egg, gap, gob, good, had, hat, it, log, lap, man, mat, net, off, pal, pay, pick, pot, ran, tab, to, wag, yam, yap, zebra,* and *zip.*

m	a	n	e	t	t	a	b	l	o	g
a	n	t	g	a	p	a	i	a	f	o
t	d	o	g	h	o	g	g	p	f	o
z	e	b	r	a	x	o	w	a	g	d
i	t	e	a	d	a	b	o	y	a	m
p	o	t	n	d	i	p	i	c	k	u

UNIT 3, LESSON 1

Long Vowels
Pages 82, 84, 89, 91, 96

I. LESSON OVERVIEW

This lesson introduces the long vowel sounds in words having the consonant-long vowel-consonant + silent *e* (CVC + *e*) spelling pattern and is a model for teaching all the long vowel sounds.

II. STUDENT OUTCOMES

The student will recognize and identify the long vowels in consonant-long vowel-consonant + silent *e* (CVC + *e*) words, and read and write CVC + *e* words.

III. PROCEDURES

Adapt the procedures in this lesson for page 82 to present all the long vowels.

Exercise A. Have the student identify the key picture *tape*. Read the key sentence, "Tape has the long a sound." Read and write other words with long *a* such as *mate, rake, pane, base,* and *cave*. (Refer to the Word List on the inside back cover for additional words.) Ask the student to suggest additional words that contain the long *a*. Write them. Point out that when words have the consonant-long vowel-consonant + silent *e* (CVC + *e*) spelling pattern, the vowel sound is usually long. Say the words and have the student repeat them emphasizing the long *a* sound. Have the student write *tape* several times in the space provided.

Exercise B. Have the student identify the pictures: *cake, box, gate, safe, inch, game, rake,* and *cage*. Have the student listen for the long *a* sound in each word and write *a* under the pictures that have the long *a* sound. Point out that the final *e* is silent.

Exercise C. Ask the student to dictate a sentence to you using at least one long *a* word. Write the sentence and read it back to the student.

Exercise D. Have students circle the words with *a_e* in the sentence from Exercise C. Then have students write the words. Have students copy the sentence in their journals.

IV. FOLLOW-UP ACTIVITIES

The following activities are designed to reinforce the student's understanding of long vowel sounds.
• Write the words: *game, came, save, cave, tape, gape, bake, lake*. Point out the consonant-long vowel-consonant + silent *e* (CVC + *e*) spelling pattern. Have students underline the long *a* in

each word. Ask students to dictate more CVC + *e* words. Write the words. Have students make flash cards of these words and read them aloud. Have students write the words in their journals.
• Ask students to listen as you read the following words: *cage, rage, lame, name, rake, take,* and *wake*. Ask students what the words have in common. Help students conclude that all the words have the long *a* sound and follow the CVC + *e* spelling pattern. Have students write the words in their journals.

UNIT 3, LESSON 2
Short Vowels and Long Vowels
Pages 83, 85, 90, 92, 97

I. LESSON OVERVIEW

This lesson compares the short vowel sounds in consonant-short vowel-consonant (CVC) words and long vowel sounds in consonant-long vowel-consonant + silent *e* (CVC + *e*) words and is a model for teaching all the short and long vowel sounds.

II. STUDENT OUTCOMES

The student will recognize and identify the short vowel sounds in consonant-short vowel-consonant (CVC) words and the long vowel sounds in consonant-long vowel-consonant + silent *e* (CVC + *e*) words, and read and write CVC and CVC + *e* words.

III. PROCEDURES

Adapt the procedures in this lesson for page 83 to review all short vowel sounds and long vowel sounds.

Exercise A. Tell the student that Exercise A reviews the short vowel sound. Remind the student that the key word *man* has the short *a* sound. Have the student identify the pictures and word choices: *fin* and *fan, bet* and *bat,* and *cat* and *cot*. Pronounce the words emphasizing the short vowel sounds. Ask the student to notice the CVC spelling pattern and recall that the vowel sound in CVC words is short. Have the student circle the words that identify the pictures and write the words in the space provided.

Exercise B. Tell the student that Exercise B reviews the long vowel sounds. Remind the student that the key word *tape* has the long *a* sound. Have the student identify the pictures and word choices: *can* and *cane*, *tap* and *tape*, *mate* and *mat*, *man* and *mane*, *cape* and *cap*, and *vane* and *van*. Pronounce the words emphasizing the long vowel sounds. Ask the student to notice the CVC + *e* spelling pattern and recall that the vowel sound in CVC + *e* words is long. Have the student circle the words that identify the pictures and write the words in the space provided.

IV. FOLLOW-UP ACTIVITIES

The following activities are designed to reinforce the student's understanding of all the short vowel sounds in CVC words and long vowel sounds in CVC + *e* words.

• Write the following words: *mad, nap, mat, wag, bit, pin,* and *sit*. Ask the student to read the words aloud. Help students identify the spelling pattern (CVC). Ask students if the vowel sound is short or long. Then have students change the spelling pattern to CVC + *e*. Have them read the words: *made, nape, mate, wage, bite, pine,* and *site*. Ask students to explain what has happened to the vowel sound. (It's changed from short to long.) Have students write the words in their journals.

• Write the word pairs: *hat* and *hate, mat* and *mate, pin* and *pine,* and *sit* and *site*. Discuss the meaning of the words. Write the following sentences:

  1. I _____ hamburgers.
     (hat, hate)
  2. Yolanda is Jim's _____ .
     (mat, mate)
  3. Sue planted a _____ tree.
     (pin, pine)
  4. My new home _____ is on Elm Street. (sit, site)

Read the sentences aloud. Ask students to choose the word that completes the meaning of each sentence. Have students write the sentences in their journal.

UNIT 3, LESSON 3

Review: Long Vowels
Pages 86, 93, 98

I. LESSON OVERVIEW

This lesson reviews long vowels in consonant-long vowel-consonant + silent *e* words and is a model for reviewing all long vowels.

II. STUDENT OUTCOMES

The student will recognize and identify long vowels in consonant-long vowel-consonant + silent *e* (CVC + *e*) words, and read and write CVC + *e* words.

III. PROCEDURES

Adapt the procedures in this lesson for page 86 to present all the review pages.

Exercise A. Review all the picture names: *cane, bike, cake, safe, hive, vine, cage,* and *rice*. Pronounce the words. Have students identify the letter for the vowel sound in each word and write the letter under the picture. Have students write the words in their journals.

Exercise B. Review the picture names and word choices: *rake* and *cake, bake; file* and *mile, tile; gate* and *date, late*. Have students circle the word that names the picture, and write it in the blank provided. Have students write the words in their journals.

IV. FOLLOW-UP ACTIVITIES

The following activities are designed to reinforce the student's understanding of all the long vowel sounds in consonant-long vowel-consonant + silent *e* words.

• Have students make flash cards for the words from Exercises A and B. Ask students to choose four of the words and make up sentences with them. Write the sentences and read them back

to students. Have students write the sentences in their journals.
• Write the following sentences and word choices:

    1. We went on a _____ .
       (hike, hide, him)
    2. I did not _____ my bike.
       (rid, ripe, ride)
    3. I _____ to hike up the hill.
       (live, like, lip)
    4. Mike likes to _____ in the lake.
       (dime, dive, dad)
    5. Kim can hike _____ miles.
       (hive, file, five)
    6. We had a good _____ .
       (tin, tame, time)

Read the sentences and the word choices aloud. Ask students to choose the word that completes the meaning of each sentence. Have students write the sentences in their journals.

UNIT 3, LESSON 4

Read a Story (Comprehension)
Pages 87, 94, 99, 101–102

I. LESSON OVERVIEW

This lesson introduces a story, frequently used sight words, and *who, what,* and *how.* Use it as a model for teaching all Read a Story pages.

II. STUDENT OUTCOMES

The student will recognize sight words, read and write words that create a story, and recall facts and details of the story.

III. PROCEDURES

Adapt the procedures in this lesson for page 87 to present all the Read a Story pages.
Introduce the sight words: *go, going, a, they, are, to, the,* and *their.* Tell the student that sight words must be memorized.
Read. Read the sentences and the word choices to the student. Ask the student to circle the word that completes the meaning of each sentence and write it in the blank. Have the student practice reading the story to you.

Think About It. Review the words *who, what,* and *how.* Then read the questions and discuss the answers with students. Tell students that the questions help them to recall facts and details of the story and to discover the main idea of the story. Ask students to suggest a title for the story. Write it. Have students copy the title and the story in their journals.

IV. FOLLOW-UP ACTIVITIES

The following activities are designed to reinforce students' recognition of sight words and their comprehension of a story.
• Have students make flash cards for the sight words: *go, going, a, they, are, to, the,* and *their.* Have students write the sight words in their journals and practice reading them.
• Have students make up another story using the same sight words and format as above (or use the example below). Write the story, read it aloud, and discuss it with students. Help students make up questions about the story using *who, what,* and *how,* and discuss the answers. Ask students to create a title for the story. Let students practice reading the story to you. Have students write the story in their journals.

    1. The time is half past _____ .
       (nine, fine, tine)
    2. Sally and Joe go on a _____ .
       (like, hike, pike)
    3. They _____ to go to the park.
       (like, site, lake)
    4. They _____ a bus to the park.
       (ride, side, rid)
    5. They are _____ if they stay on the trail. (late, safe, make)
    6. They hike _____ miles.
       (hive, dive, five)

  ©Steck-Vaughn Co. *Reading for Today Instructor's Guide.* No part of this document may be reproduced without written permission from Steck-Vaughn.

UNIT 3, LESSON 5

Read and Write
(Language Experience Activity)
Pages 88, 95, 100

I. LESSON OVERVIEW

This lesson introduces Read and Write, which is a language experience activity (LEA), and is a model for teaching all the Read and Write pages in Unit Three.

II. STUDENT OUTCOMES

Students will apply their knowledge of letter-sound associations for long vowels in the context of words to create a story.

III. PROCEDURES

Adapt the procedures in this lesson to present all the Read and Write pages.

The language experience activity lets students use their own experience and words to create a story.

Exercise A. Read the words: *tape, kite, bike, cane, fine,* and *cape*. Ask the student to suggest relationships among some of the words such as *tape* and *kite*.

Exercise B. Have the student copy the words. Ask the student to choose the words that he or she can connect in a story.

Exercise C. (Language Experience Activity) Have the student tell a story or describe an experience using one or more of the words from Exercise B. (See the example story below.) Write the story exactly as the student tells it. Read the story back to the student and discuss it together.

Exercise D. Ask the student to think of a title for the story. Have the student copy the story in the journal and practice reading it to you. Example story:

> Judy got a kite for her tenth birthday. She rode her bike to the park where she could fly her kite. Judy ran fast to get the kite into the air. It kept falling to the ground. An older woman thought the kite was blowing away, so she stabbed it with her cane. Judy rode her bike home and repaired the kite with some tape.

IV. FOLLOW-UP ACTIVITIES

The following activities are designed to reinforce the student's understanding of letter-sound associations for long vowels in the context of words in a story.

• Read the words *ice, dive, time, face, came, late, wade, lake,* and *fire*. Ask students to copy the words and choose the ones they can use to create a story. Have students tell you a story. Write the story and read it back to students. Have students copy the story in their journals and practice reading it to you. Have students make up a title by asking *Who?, What?,* and *Why?* questions about the story. Have them write the title above the story.

• Have students bring in a story for you to read aloud. Discuss the story with students and help them pick out clues about the story's main idea by asking questions beginning with *Who, What,* and *Why*. Have students write the questions and possible answers in their journals as models for thinking about future stories.

UNIT 3, LESSON 6

End of Unit Review
Pages 103–104

I. LESSON OVERVIEW

The lesson reviews and assesses the student's grasp of the letter-sound associations for long vowels in consonant-long vowel-consonant + silent *e* (CVC + *e*) words. Use this lesson as a review or as a test.

II. STUDENT OUTCOMES

The student will recognize all long vowels in consonant-long vowel-consonant + silent *e* (CVC + *e*) words, and read and write CVC + *e* words.

III. PROCEDURES

Review a, ee, i, o, and u. Ask the student to identify the pictures on page 103: *bone, cake, tube, vine, cone, cane, jeep, feet, note, weed, home,* and *rice*. Below each picture, have the student write the letter that completes each word. Have the student read the words to you. Check the student's work.

Review a, ea, i, o, and u. Have the student identify the pictures on page 104: *bike, five, rake, stove, cube, leaf, hose, safe, robe, fuse, kite,* and *cape.* Below each picture, have the student write the letter that completes each word. Have the student read the words to you. Check the student's work.

IV. FOLLOW-UP ACTIVITIES

The following activities are designed to reteach and enrich the student's understanding of letter-sound associations for long vowels.

• If the student cannot recognize and identify some of the vowel sounds, ask the student to use the flash cards to review the sounds. Have the student identify the key picture names for each long vowel. Review the consonant-long vowel-consonant + silent *e* spelling pattern. Remind the student that the vowel in CVC + *e* word is usually long.

• Read the following riddles to the student. Have him or her say the words that the clues suggest.

1. It begins like *cake* and rhymes with *drape.* (cape)
2. It begins like *tire* and rhymes with *cake.* (take)
3. It begins like *dog* and rhymes with *five.* (dive)
4. It begins like *ride* and rhymes with *wake.* (rake)
5. It begins like *late* and rhymes with *bake.* (lake)

• Write the following nonsense words: *jok, pok, hol, pol, hom, doz,* and *vot.* Guide students to tell you that the words become meaningful when a silent *e* is added (CVC + *e*). Have students read the long vowel words and write them in their journals.

• Have the student search for words in the puzzle below. The words are written forward and up and down. Some words overlap. Look

for these words: *bone, net, tape, bike, note, peak, hose, doze, seek, feet, teem, eat, wage, date, ate, cape,* and *rice.*

b	o	n	e	t	t	a	p	e	o	h
i	n	o	t	e	p	e	a	k	f	o
k	d	o	z	e	o	g	g	p	f	s
e	a	t	r	m	x	o	w	a	g	e
f	e	e	t	d	a	t	e	a	t	e
c	a	p	e	r	i	c	e	c	k	k

Final Review
Pages 105–107

I. LESSON OVERVIEW

The lesson reviews and assesses the student's recognition and identification of initial and final consonants and long and short vowels. Use this lesson as a review or as a test.

II. STUDENT OUTCOMES

The student will identify words with initial and final consonants and long and short vowels.

III. PROCEDURES

Have the student identify the pictures on page 105: *hug, vane, gate, tax, ant, meat, jam, six, hole, nest, cap,* and *jet.* Have the student read the words to you. Below each picture, have the student write the letter that completes each word. Check the student's work.

Have the student identify the pictures on page 106: *rod, bus, cube, pot, dam, mail, zoo, bike, win, bat, gum,* and *cage.* Have the student read the words to you. Below each picture, have the student write the letter that completes each word. Check the student's work.

Have the student identify the pictures on page 107: *tub, file, men, hive, yarn, fin, kite, web, leaf, quart, bone,* and *sun.* Have the student read the words to you. Below each picture, have the student write the letter that completes each word. Check the student's work.

IV. FOLLOW-UP ACTIVITIES

The following activities are designed to reteach and enrich the student's recognition and identification of letter-sound associations for all letters of the alphabet.

• If the student cannot recognize and identify some of the consonants and vowel sounds, have the student use flash cards to review the sounds. Have the student identify the key picture names for each consonant and vowel.

• Show students flash cards at random. Have students identify the word or letter on each card and make up a sentence using it. Write the sentences and read them back to students. Have students copy the additional sentences in their journals.

Book One

Overview

Book One is designed for the adult student who can recognize and write the letters of the alphabet and has had some prior exposure to reading. Written at the .5–1.0 reading level, Book One uses adult vocabulary, photos, and situations to teach words in the context of phrases, sentences, and stories. The book may be used as a continuation for students who have mastered the material in the Introductory Book, or as a starting point of instruction for students who placed out of that level.

Book One has two main objectives: to review the phonics skills covered in the Introductory Book, and to teach the most common sight words. These basic words include high-frequency nouns and verbs as well as function words such as *a, the, was, of, with, for, this,* and *you.* Most of these basic words are not phonetically regular and must be memorized. Book One presents the sight words in a variety of word groupings with interesting photo settings to add context and relevance to adults.

The sight words in Book One were selected from the following word lists: the Dolch Basic Sight Vocabulary, the EDL Core Vocabularies, the Mitzel Functional Reading Word List for Adults, the Kuçera-Francis List, and the Madden-Carlson 250 Words of Highest Frequency in Our Language.

Unit 1 is a phonics unit that reviews the consonant sounds.

Unit 2, also a phonics unit, reviews short and long vowel sounds in the consonant-vowel-consonant and consonant-vowel-consonant + silent *e* patterns.

Unit 3 teaches sight words and combines them in short phrases such as *a big dog* and in short sentences such as *The man runs.* The student also practices word building by adding the endings *–s, –es, –ed,* and *–ing* to known sight words. Each lesson includes a review, and each unit ends with a comprehensive review that may be used as a mastery test.

Unit 4 teaches function words such as *a, the, and, not* and number words. A Final Review assesses the student's mastery of the skills presented throughout the book.

Book One emphasizes the reading-writing connection by encouraging students to keep a personal journal. The journal is a place where students can compile vocabulary lists of all kinds, practice writing sentences and answering questions, and record their stories and personal observations.

The reading/writing connection is strongest in the Read a Story lesson on pages 105–106. The story deals with a situation common to adult students and uses many of the words in Book One. Based on the title and photos as well as their prior knowledge, students predict what the story is about. After reading the story, students summarize the events. The section Think About It poses *who, where, when, what,* and *why* questions that determine the student's comprehension of the story. The questions can be used as a basis for discussion. This activity prepares the student for the longer reading selections in Book Two.

Word List. A master Word List of all the words introduced in this book is on the inside back cover.

Workbook One provides additional practice of the skills taught in Book One. As the student completes a unit in Book One, the instructor should assign the corresponding unit in the workbook.

UNIT 1, LESSON 1

Reviewing Consonant Sounds
Pages 1, 2, 3, 4, 5

I. LESSON OVERVIEW

This lesson reviews initial and final consonant sounds. Use the lesson as a model for reviewing all initial and final consonants.

II. STUDENT OUTCOMES

The student will recognize and identify initial and final consonant sounds, and read and write words with initial and final consonants.

III. PROCEDURES

Adapt the procedures in this lesson for page 1 to review all the initial and final consonants.

Page 1, Exercise A. Write and read the letters and key words: *d* in *dog*, *b* in *bee*, *f* in *leaf*, and *c* in *cat*. Have the student say each picture name: *dog, bee, leaf, cat, fork, tub, cup, food, cow, web, fan*, and *door*. Have the student listen for the sound and write the missing letter in the blank.

Exercise B. Have the student write any two words that begin with *b* or *c*. The student may choose words from Exercise A or think of others. (For more example words, see the Word List on the inside back cover.)

Journal. You may want to have the student write the words in Exercise B in a journal. Encourage each student to start a journal and write in it daily. The journal might be divided into sections for vocabulary, sample sentences, and creative writing. Encourage the student to make writing in the journal an ongoing activity.

Exercise C. Have the student write any two words that begin with *d* or *f*. The student may choose words from Exercise A or think of others. (For more example words, see the Word List on the inside back cover.) Have the student write the words in the journal.

IV. FOLLOW-UP ACTIVITIES

The following activities are designed to reinforce the student's understanding of consonant sounds.

• Have the student make flash cards of the words from the exercises on page 1. Then ask him or her to dictate a sentence to you using each word. Write the sentences and read them aloud. Have the student copy the sentences in the journal.
• Have the student bring a department or specialty store catalog. Ask the student to draw circles around the objects beginning with the letters *b, c, d*, or *f (bookshelf, car mats, door rack, or food processor).*
• Help the student plan a party using foods and party items beginning with the letters *b, c, d*, or *f*. Help the student to suggest items such as *brownies, cake, chips and dips*, and *fruit*. Write the words and read them back. Have the student copy the words in the journal.
• Ask the student to look around the room for objects beginning with *b, c, d*, or *f*. Write the words. Ask the student to make up a sentence using one or more of the words. Write the sentence and read it back. Have the student read the sentence and copy it in the journal.

V. WORKBOOK

Assign Workbook One, Unit 1, pages 4–9.

UNIT 2, LESSON 1

Review Short Vowel Sounds
Pages 6, 9, 13, 16, 20

I. LESSON OVERVIEW

This lesson reviews short vowel sounds. Most of the words with short vowel sounds have the consonant-short vowel-consonant (CVC) spelling pattern. Use the lesson as a model for reviewing all short vowels.

II. STUDENT OUTCOMES

The student will recognize and identify the short vowel sounds and read and write words with short vowels.

III. PROCEDURES

Adapt the procedures in this lesson for page 6 to present all the short vowels in Unit Two.

Exercise A. Write and read the letter *a* and the key word *apple*. Have the student say each picture name: *apple, cat, jam, mat, cap, pan, can, ant, van, map, bat,* and *hat.* Have the student listen for the sound and write the missing letter in the blank.

Exercise B. Have the student write any two words with the short *a* sound. The student may choose words from Exercise A or think of others. (For more example words, see the Word List on the inside back cover.)

Journal. You may want to have the student write the words in Exercise B in a journal. Encourage each student to start a journal and write in it daily. The journal might be divided into sections for vocabulary, sample sentences, and creative writing. Encourage the student to make writing in the journal an ongoing activity.

IV. FOLLOW-UP ACTIVITIES

The following activities are designed to reinforce the student's understanding of the short vowel sounds in CVC words.

• Have the student make flash cards of the words from Exercises A and B on page 6. Then ask him or her to dictate a sentence to you using each word. Write the sentences and read them aloud. Have the student copy the sentences in the journal.

• Introduce the student to four word families: *–am, –ab, –ad,* and *–ag.* Write the family names. Have the student add initial consonants to the family names to spell words: *d–am, h–am, j–ab, c–ab, p–ad, b–ag, l–ag.* Point out the consonant-short vowel-consonant (CVC) spelling pattern. Ask the student to dictate more CVC words for each family. Write each word under the appropriate family group. Have the student make flash cards of these words and read them aloud.

• Ask the student to listen as you read the following words from the *–ag* word family: *bag,* rag, tag, and wag. Ask the student what the words have in common. Help the student conclude that all the words have the medial short *a* sound and all the words sound alike (rhyme). Now read another list of words: *bad, dad, dog.* Ask the student what is different about this group. Help the student conclude that *dog* does not sound like the other words because it has a different vowel sound.

• Ask the student to bring something he or she wants to read. Have the student scan for words that begin with the short *a.* Read the sentence containing the short *a* word to the student. Ask the student to read it back to you. Then have the student copy the sentence and circle the short *a* words.

UNIT 2, LESSON 2

Review Long Vowel Sounds
Pages 7, 10, 14, 17

I. LESSON OVERVIEW

This lesson reviews long vowel sounds. Most of the words with long vowel sounds have the consonant-long vowel-consonant + silent *e* (CVC + *e*) spelling pattern. Use this lesson as a model for reviewing all the long vowel sounds.

II. STUDENT OUTCOMES

The student will recognize and identify the long vowel sounds and read and write words with long vowels.

III. PROCEDURES

Adapt the procedures in this lesson for page 7 to review all the long vowels in Unit Two.

Exercise A. Have the student say each picture name: *tape, cake, rake, cage, gate, safe, cape, vane, cane, game, vase, pane.* Have him or her write the missing letters under each picture. Point out the CVC + *e* spelling pattern in *tape* and *cake.* Be sure the student knows that the final *e* is silent.

Exercise B. Have the student write any two words with long vowel *a_e.* sound. The student may choose words from Exercise A or think of others. (For more example words, see the Word List on the inside back cover.) Have the student write the words in the journal.

FOLLOW-UP ACTIVITIES

The following activities are designed to reinforce the student's understanding of long vowel sounds in CVC·+ *e* words.

• Have the student make flash cards of the words from Exercises A and B on page 7. Then ask him or her to dictate a sentence to you using at least one long *a_e* word. Write the sentence and read it back. Have the student circle the words with *a_e* in the sentence. Then have the student write the words. Have the student copy the sentence in the journal.

• Ask the student to bring something he or she wants to read. Have the student scan for words with the long *a* sound. Read the sentence containing the long *a* word to the student. Ask the student to read it back to you. Then have the student copy the sentence and circle the long *a* words.

• Write the words: *game, came, save, cave, tape, gape, bake, lake.* Point out the consonant-long vowel-consonant + silent *e* (CVC + *e*) spelling pattern. Have students underline the long *a* in each word. Ask students to dictate more CVC + *e* words. Write the words. Have students make flash cards of these words and read them aloud. Have students write the words in their journals.

• Ask the student to look at each word in Exercise A and decide if it is a CVC + *e* word by writing *c* over consonants and *v* over vowels. Do the first word together. Have the student circle the long vowel in each word and underline the final silent *e*. Then have the student write the words in the journal.

UNIT 2, LESSON 3
Review Short and Long Vowel Sounds
Pages 8, 11, 15, 18, 22

I. LESSON OVERVIEW
This lesson reviews the difference between words with the consonant-short vowel-consonant (CVC) spelling pattern and those with the consonant-long vowel-consonant + silent *e* (CVC + *e*) pattern. Use this lesson as a model for teaching all CVC and CVC + *e* words.

II. STUDENT OUTCOMES
The student will recognize and identify short vowels in CVC words and long vowels in CVC + *e* words, and read and write CVC and CVC + *e* words.

III. PROCEDURES
Adapt the procedures in this lesson for page 8 to present all the long and short vowels.
Exercise A. Have the student listen for the long and short vowels as you read the picture names and word choices: *tap* and *tape, mate* and *mat, can* and *cane, mane* and *man, cap* and *cape, vane* and *van, hate* and *hat, am* and *ace,* and *pane* and *pan.* Remind him or her that the vowel sound in CVC words is short and the vowel in CVC + *e* words is long. Have the student circle the picture name, write it in the blank, and the write the words in the journal.
Exercise B. Have the student write a sentence with a long *a* word from Exercise A. Read the sentence aloud and have the student write it in the journal.
Exercise C. Have the student write a sentence with a short *a* word from Exercise A. Read the sentence aloud and have the student write it in the journal.

FOLLOW-UP ACTIVITIES
The following activities are designed to reinforce the student's recognition of short vowels in CVC words and long vowels in CVC + *e* words.

• Have the student make flash cards of the words in Exercise A. Then ask him or her to dictate a sentence using each word. Write the sentences and read them back. Have the student copy the sentences in the journal.

• Ask the student to look at each word in Exercise A and decide if it is a CVC or a CVC + e word by writing c over consonants and v over vowels. Do the first word together. Have the student circle the short vowel in CVC words and underline the vowel in CVC + e words and write the words in the journal.

UNIT 2, LESSON 4

Read a Story (Comprehension)
Pages 12, 23

I.   LESSON OVERVIEW

This lesson introduces a story using long vowels previously reviewed and sight words. Use this lesson as a model for teaching all Read a Story pages in Unit Two.

II.   STUDENT OUTCOMES

The student will read CVC + e words in context and recall details of the story.

III.   PROCEDURES

Adapt the procedures in this lesson for page 12 to present all the Read a Story pages.
Introduce the sight words: *kite, pine, hive, came, race, time*. Tell the student that these sight words must be memorized through repeated practice.
Exercise A.   Read each sentence and the three word choices with the student. Discuss the story together. Ask the student to circle the word that best completes each sentence and write it in the blank. Have the student practice reading the story to you.
Exercise B.   Read the questions and discuss the answers together. Remind the student that a story's title provides a clue about the main idea of the story. Ask the student to suggest a title for the story. Write it. Have the student copy the story in the journal.

IV.   FOLLOW-UP ACTIVITIES

The following activities are designed to reinforce the student's recognition of reading CVC + e words and sight words and comprehension of a story.
• Have the students make flash cards for the sight words: *kite, pine, hive, came, race,* and *time*. Have the student write the sight words in the journal and practice reading them.
• Have the student make up another story using the same sight words and format on page 12. Write the story, read it aloud, and discuss it together. Ask the student to write a title for the story. Let him or her practice reading the story to you. Have the student write the story in the journal.

UNIT 2, LESSON 5

Reading Sentences
Page 19

I.   LESSON OVERVIEW

This lesson introduces sentences using CVC + e words and sight words.

II.   STUDENT OUTCOMES

The student will read CVC + e words in context, recognize sight words, and write words that complete sentences.

III.   PROCEDURES

Exercise A.   Review the sight words: *mule, nose, home, fuse, hole,* and *bone.* Tell the student that he or she must memorize sight words through repeated practice. Read the first pair of sentences and the word choices with the student. Discuss the pairs of sentences as questions and answers. Ask the student to circle the word that best completes each sentence and write it in the blank. Have the student practice reading the sentence pairs to you.

IV.   FOLLOW-UP ACTIVITIES

The following activities are designed to reinforce the student's recognition of CVC + e words and sight words and comprehension of sentences.

• Have the students make flash cards for the sight words: *mule, nose, home, fuse, hole, and bone.* Have the student write the sight words in the journal.

• Have the student make up pairs of sentences (such as the ones below) using the same words and format as Exercise A. Write the story and read it aloud. Then discuss it together. Let him or her practice reading the story to you. Have the student write the story in the journal.

1. How can you get a _____ to move?
   can   dog   cane
2. You can pull it by the _____ .
   leash   tone   zone

UNIT 2, LESSON 6

Review Long Vowel *e* Spelled *ee* and *ea*
Page 21

I.   LESSON OVERVIEW

This lesson reviews the long *e* vowel sound spelled *ee* and *ea.*

II.   STUDENT OUTCOMES

The student will recognize and identify the long *e* vowel sound spelled *ee* and *ea,* and read and write words with the long *e* spelled *ee* and *ea.*

III.   PROCEDURES

Exercise A.   Have the student listen as you review the picture names: *leaf, bee, jeep, seal, feet, meat, weed, tea, sea, seed, queen,* and *team.* Point out that the long *e* vowel sound can be spelled *ee* as in *bee* or *ea* in *leaf.* Ask him or her to write the missing letter in the blank. Then have the student write the words in the journal.

Exercise B.   Have the student write two words with long *e* spelled *ea.* The student may choose words from Exercise A or think of others. (For more example words, see the Word List on the inside back cover.) Have the student write the words in the journal.

Exercise C.   Have the student write two words with long *e* spelled *ee.* The student may choose

words from Exercise A or think of others. (For more example words, see the Word List on the inside back cover.) Have the student write the words in the journal.

IV.   FOLLOW-UP ACTIVITIES

The following activities are designed to reinforce the student's understanding of the long *e* vowel sound spelled *ee* and *ea.*

• Have the student make flash cards of the words from Exercises A, B, and C. Ask the student to dictate two sentences to you, one with a long *e* spelled *ee* word and one with a long *e* spelled *ea.* Write the sentences and read them back. Have the student circle the words with *ee* or *ea.* Then have him or her write the words. Have the student copy the sentences in the journal.

• Write the words: *bead, week, peek, beam, read, weep,* and *deer.* Have the student underline the long *e* spelled *ee* or *ea* in each word. Ask the student to dictate more *ee* or *ea* words. (For more examples, see the Word List on the inside back cover.) Write the words. Have him or her make flash cards of all the words and read them aloud. Have the student write the words in the journal.

V.   WORKBOOK

Assign Workbook One, Unit 2, pages 10–19.

UNIT 3, LESSON 1

Sight Words
Pages 24–27, 32–35, 40–43, 48–53

I.   LESSON OVERVIEW

This lesson introduces five new sight words: *big, man, run, sit,* and *stand.* Use this lesson as a model for teaching all the sight words in Unit Three.

II.   STUDENT OUTCOMES

The student will recognize, read, and write the five new sight words.

III. PROCEDURES

Teach each two-page sight word section as one lesson. Adapt the procedures in this lesson for pages 24–27 to present all the new sight words in Unit Three.

Page 24, Exercise A. Read the five sight words to the student: *big, man, run, sit,* and *stand.* Have the student repeat the words. Give an example sentence for each word.

Exercise B. Discuss the photo together. Have the student identify the objects and actions and read the five new words printed on the photo. Ask the student to predict what the story below might be about based on seeing the photo and five new words.

Exercise C. Read the story aloud as the student follows along. Have him or her circle the sight words in the story. Have the student think of a word that means the opposite of *big* (*little*) and *sit* (*stand*).

Page 25, Exercise A. Have the student reread the sight words on page 24. Have him or her look at the picture for help in recognizing the words.

Exercise B. Tell the student that the only possible answers for Exercises B and C are the five new words. Then have him or her write the missing letter in each word and write the word on the line below. Have the student make flash cards for each word.

Alternate Exercise B, page 49. Say each word. Then have the student say the sight word that rhymes and write it on the line.

Exercise C. Have the student write the word that identifies each photo. Then have him or her read the words to you.

Alternate Exercise C, pages 27, 33, 41, 43 and 53. Tell the student that the only possible answers for Exercise C are the five new words. Then read each sentence aloud and have the student write the missing word in each sentence.

Exercise D, pages 27, 33, 41, 43 and 53. Have the student write a sentence with each of

the new words. Help the student with any other words he or she needs.

Alternate Exercise D, page 51. Have the student write a sentence with one of the new words. Help the student with any other words he or she needs.

IV. FOLLOW-UP ACTIVITIES

The following activities are designed to reinforce the student's mastery of sight words.

• Have the student write the new sight words in the journal. You might want him or her to make a section just for sight words. Explain that many sight words are not phonetically regular and the student must memorize them. However these sight words are regular.

• Dictate the five new words and have the student write them. Ask him or her to identify the beginning consonant sound of each word and underline the letter that stands for the sound. Point out that in *stand* the letters *s* and *t* are sounded together. Ask the student to think of other words that begin with the *st* sound (*stop, store, step, stick*).

• Ask the student to point out the action words in the story (*run, stand, and sit*). Have him or her think of words that mean the opposite of these words (*walk, sit, and stand*). Then have the student think of words that mean the same as *run* (*jog, trot*).

• Draw word configuration boxes in the shape of the letters in each new word.

Example: big =

Have the student fill in the boxes while looking at the new words on page 24.

UNIT 3, LESSON 2

Writing Skills—Action Words
Pages 28, 44, 54

I. LESSON OVERVIEW

This lesson introduces the inflectional endings *–s, –es, –ed,* and *–ing* added to verbs. Use this lesson as a model for teaching all the Writing Skills lessons in Unit Three.

II. STUDENT OUTCOMES

The student will add the inflectional endings *–s, –es, –ed,* and *–ing* to previously-learned action words.

III. PROCEDURES

Adapt the procedures in this lesson for page 28 to present all the Writing Skills lessons in Unit Three.

Exercise A.   Ask the student to read the words in Exercise A: *run, go, sit, do, stand, watch, stop* and *fix.* Ask what is alike about these words. (They are action words or verbs.) Explain that words ending in a vowel, *ch,* or *x* add *–es* instead of *–s.* Have the student add *–s* or *–es* to each word, using the first word, *run,* as a model, and write the new words. Have the student read the words aloud and then write them in the journal. Make up sentences using the new words.

Exercise B.   Read the sentences aloud and have the student read them back to you. Discuss the action in the photo and ask him or her to underline the sentence that tells about the picture. Ask the student why the other sentences are incorrect (because the man does not stop, stand, or sit).

Exercise C.   Read the story while the student looks at the picture. Have the student write the missing letters.

Alternate Exercise C, pages 45 and 55.   Read each sentence together. Have the student read the words in the word box. Then have him or her write the word that completes each sentence.

Exercise D.   Have the student write the word that identifies each photo. Then have him or her read the words to you.

Alternate Exercise D, page 45.   Look at each picture and discuss it together. Read the sentences aloud as the student follows along. Have the student underline the sentence that

goes with the picture. Have him or her read the answers to you.

IV. FOLLOW-UP ACTIVITIES

The following activities are designed to reinforce the student's mastery of reading words with the inflectional ending *–s.*

• Write *I run* and *You run.* Read the sentences aloud, and have the student read them back to you. Then ask the student to look at Exercise B on page 28 and substitute *He* for *A man.* Write *He run.* Read it aloud and ask what is wrong with the sentence (*run* needs *–s* added). Have the student look at the sentence again and substitute *She* for *He.* Write *She run* and ask what letter should be added to *run (–s).* Have the student write the sentences in the journal.

• Write a word from Exercise A on page 28 and circle the root word. Explain that a root word is the word without the ending. Ask him or her to circle the root word for the other words in Exercise A.

• Point out that in Exercise B the student is reading complete sentences. Explain that a sentence states a complete idea, begins with a capital letter and ends with a period. Ask the student to write four new sentences like the ones in Exercise B using *go, do, watch,* and *fix* instead of *run, stop, stand,* and *sit.*

UNIT 3, LESSON 3

Writing Skills—Naming Words
Pages 36–37

I. LESSON OVERVIEW

This lesson introduces the inflectional endings *–s* and *–es* added to nouns.

II. STUDENT OUTCOMES

The student will add the inflectional endings *–s* and *–es* to previously-learned naming words.

III. PROCEDURES

Exercise A.   Ask the student to read the words

in Exercise A: *home, ranch, key, grass, dog, boss, table, box,* and *radio.* Ask what is alike about these words. (They are naming words or nouns.) Explain that words ending in *ch, s,* or *x* add *–es* instead of *–s.* Have the student add *–s* or *–es* to each word, using the first word, *home,* as a model, and write the new words. Have the student read the words aloud and then write them in the journal. Make up sentences using the new words.

Exercise B. Read the sentences aloud and have the student read them back to you. Discuss the action in the photo and ask him or her to underline the sentence that tells about the picture. Ask the student why the other sentences are incorrect (because the person in the picture is a woman, and she is buying tables, not stopping dogs).

Exercise C. Have the student write the word that identifies each photo. Then have him or her read the words to you.

UNIT 3, LESSON 4

Review of Sight Words
Pages 30–31, 38–39, 46–47, 56–57

I.   LESSON OVERVIEW

This lesson reviews ten new sight words: *big, man, run, sit, stand, can, go, stop, food,* and *table.* Use this lesson as a model for all the sight word review pages in Unit Three.

II.   STUDENT OUTCOMES

The student will recognize, read, and write ten previously-taught sight words.

III.   PROCEDURES

Adapt the procedures in this lesson for page 30 to review all the sight words in Unit Three. Write the ten sight words for pages 24–27: *big, man, run, sit, stand, can, go, stop, food,* and *table.* Read the words aloud as the student follows along. Then read the words together.

Exercise A.   Discuss each picture together. Have the student read the word choices beneath each picture. Then have him or her write the word that goes with the picture and read the word.

Exercise B.   Look at each picture and discuss it together. Read the sentences aloud as the student follows along. Have the student underline the sentence that goes with the picture. Have him or her read the answers to you.

Exercise C.   Read the sentences aloud and have the student read them back to you. Discuss the action in the photo and ask him or her to underline the sentence that tells about the picture. Ask the student why the other sentences are incorrect (because the woman does not go, fix, or do).

Alternative Exercise C, page 47.   Read each sentence together. Have the student read the words in the word box. Then have him or her write the word that completes each sentence.

Alternative Exercise C, page 57.   Read the story while the student looks at the picture. Have the student write the missing words.

Exercise D.   Have the student add *–s* or *–es* to each word and write the new words.

IV.   FOLLOW-UP ACTIVITIES

The following activities are designed to reinforce the student's mastery of ten previously-taught sight words.

• Have the student make up a sentence with each of the sight words. Have him or her circle the sight word in each sentence.

• Show the student sight word flash cards at random. Have the student read each word and give a sentence using the word. Have the student write the words in the journal.

• Dictate several sight words. Have the student write the words. Then have him or her tell you some other words that start with the same letter. (For additional words, see the Word List on the inside back cover.)

• Have the student circle the sight words in the word search below. The words may be written forward, backward, and up and down.

```
r   u   n   b   i   g   s
m   o   s   i   t   a   t
a   c   a   n   w   x   a
n   p   o   t   s   e   n
t   a   b   l   e   w   d
p   g   o   d   o   o   f
```

UNIT 3, LESSON 5

End of Unit Review
Page 58–59

I.   LESSON OVERVIEW

This lesson reviews and assesses the student's mastery of the 45 sight words presented in Unit Three.

II.   STUDENT OUTCOMES

The student will recognize, read, and write the new sight words in lists and in sentence context.

III.   PROCEDURES

Exercise A.   Review the 45 sight words covered in Unit 3 by turning to pages 24, 26, 32, 34, 40, 42, 48, 50, and 52 and reading the words together. Then read the words in the word box and the directions for the exercise. Have the student fill in the missing letters in the words independently. Check the student's work.

Exercise B.   Read each sentence together. Have the student read the words in the word box. Then have him or her write the word that completes each sentence.

Exercise C.   Have the student add –s or –es to each word and write the new word. Check the student's work.

Exercise D.   Have the student add –ed to each word and write the new word. Check the student's work.

Exercise E.   Have the student add –ing to each word and write the new word. Check the student's work.

IV.   FOLLOW-UP ACTIVITIES

The following activities are designed to reinforce the student's mastery of the 45 sight words presented in Unit 3.

• Have the student make up a sentence with each of the sight words: *man, run, food, stop, use, walk, buy, radio, nurse,* and *boss.* Have him or her circle the sight word in each sentence.

• Show the student sight word flash cards at random. Have the student read the word and say what letter sound it begins with. Have the student make up a sentence with each word and write the sentence in the journal.

• Dictate several sight words. Have the student write the words. Then have him or her think of other words that start with the same letter. (For additional words, see the Word List on the inside back cover.) Ask the student to use several words in sentences and write them in the journal.

• Have the student look at the words in parentheses, and then read the sentences. Have him or her write the word that completes each sentence.

1. The _____ is in the repair shop. (radio, boss)
2. James's _____ is green. (van, sister)
3. _____ like to sit in the park. (People, Light)
4. This is the _____ to my door. (bed, key)
5. Do you have enough _____ to _____ the car? (family, money) (run, buy)
6. A sick person needs a _____ . (nurse, get)
7. At work my supervisor is a _____ . (table, woman)
8. Be sure to _____ at the right house! (stop, run)
9. I am my brother's _____ . (sister, store)
10. Lori pays the _____ each month. (walk, bills)

• Have the student write the missing letter in the following sight words.

1. b _ ss	2. broth _ r
3. c _ ty	4. _ urse
5. wor _	6. w _ lk
7. j _ b	8. f _ _ d
9. h _ me	10. p _ _ ple

• Have the student circle the sight words in the word search below. The words may be written forward, backward, or up and down. Some words overlap. These words are in the puzzle: *car, table, can, pay, key, use, people, job, boss, van, stop, yell, family, sit,* and *look.*

c	a	n	k	e	y	p	a	y
a	t	a	b	l	e	e	s	u
r	u	n	b	o	j	o	l	y
n	a	v	o	s	e	p	o	e
t	a	b	s	e	w	l	o	l
p	o	t	s	o	o	e	k	l
f	a	m	i	l	y	s	i	t

V. WORKBOOK

Assign Workbook One, Unit 3, pages 20–29.

UNIT 4, LESSON 1

More Sight Words
Pages 60–64, 74–78, 88–90

I. LESSON OVERVIEW

This lesson introduces six new sight words: *a, an, the, and, he,* and *she.* These words are also called "function words" because they are not easily pictured but are vital to forming sentences. Use this lesson as a model for teaching all the sight words in Unit Four.

II. STUDENT OUTCOMES

The student will recognize, read, and write the new sight words.

III. PROCEDURES

Adapt the procedures in this lesson for pages 60–61 to present all the new sight words in Unit Four.

Page 60, Exercise A. Read aloud the three sight words: *a, an,* and *the.* Have the student repeat the words. Point out that these words are not easy to show in pictures but are used in almost every sentence we read. Then have him or her identify the pictures and read the phrase beneath each. Explain that *a man* refers to any man and *the man* refers to a specific man. Have the student write a sentence with each phrase in the journal.

Exercise B. Identify the photos together. Ask the student if the picture names begin with a consonant or a vowel. Explain that *an* is used with words that begin with the vowels *a, e, i, o,* and *u.* Say the words *an apple, an egg,* and *an umbrella* as the student listens. Have him or her repeat the phrases. Then have the student write the phrases in the journal.

Page 61, Exercise A. Read the new words: *and, he,* and *she.* Discuss the photos together and have the student describe what is happening in each. Point out that each photo is numbered to go with a set of sentences. Then read the four sets of sentences aloud, and have the student read them back to you. Point out that the words in dark type are the new words. Ask the student to reread the sentences and point out the personal pronouns that take the place of the people's names *(he, she).*

Alternative Exercise A, pages 88, 89, and 90. Read the new words: *your, so,* and *very.* Discuss the photos together and have the student describe what he or she sees in each. Then read the sentences aloud, and have the student read them back to you. Have the student write the new word or words from the sentence.

Exercise B. Read the groups of sentences aloud, and have the student read them back to you. Then have him or her find the new words in the sentences and write the words.

Alternative Exercise B, pages 88, 89, and 90. Read the groups of sentences aloud, and have the student read them back to you. Then have him or her underline the new words.

IV. FOLLOW-UP ACTIVITIES

The following activities are designed to reinforce the student's mastery of sight words.

• Have the student make flash cards for the new sight words. Then have him or her pick out other flash cards of action words and combine them with the new flash cards to make sentences. Have the student write the sentences in the journal and circle the new sight words.

• Dictate the following words: *ax, wax, vest, olive, uncle, map, elbow,* and *inch.* Have the student write *a* before naming words that begin with consonants and *an* before naming words beginning with the vowels *a, e, i, o,* and *u.* Ask him or her to make up a sentence with each phrase.

• Write the following sentences:
  Julie cooks.
  Jeff cooks.
  Julie and Jeff cook.

Have the student substitute the personal pronouns *he* and *she* for the names in the sentences. Ask him or her to think of a personal pronoun that can take the place of both names in the last sentence *(they).* Explain that *they* is a plural personal pronoun. Have the student write the sentences and personal pronouns in the journal.

• Point out that in the word *the,* the letters *t* and *h* combined stand for a new sound (not a blend), also in *this, that, they.* Dictate *take, talk, this, that, tag,* and *they.* Have the student listen to the difference in beginning sounds between the *t* and the *th* words. Have him or her write the words in the journal.

UNIT 4, LESSON 2

Review of Sight Words
Pages 65–66, 79–80, and 91

I. LESSON OVERVIEW

This lesson reviews the sight words: *a, an, the, and, he, she, is, was, are, were, I, you, they,* *this, that,* and *it.* Use this lesson as a model for all the Review pages in Unit Four.

II. STUDENT OUTCOMES

The student will recognize, identify, read, and write fifteen previously-taught sight words.

III. PROCEDURES

Adapt the procedures in this lesson for pages 65–66 to review all the sight words in Unit Four.
Page 65, Exercise A. Discuss each picture. Then ask the student to read the sentence and the word choices that go with the picture. Have him or her write the word that makes sense in the context of the sentence. Ask the student to read the complete sentence and write it in the journal.
Page 66, Exercise B. Have the student read the words in the word box, and then read the sentences that go with each box. Ask him or her to write the word that best completes each sentence.
Exercise C. Read the paragraph aloud as the student listens. Ask him or her to read it back to you. Explain that a paragraph is a group of sentences telling about one idea or topic. Ask the student what the main idea of this paragraph is (the modes of travel of several people). Point out that the first line of a paragraph is indented. Have the student read the words in the word box and underline the new words in the paragraph. Then have the student write the paragraph in the journal.

IV. FOLLOW-UP ACTIVITIES

The following activities are designed to reinforce the student's mastery of sight words.
• Write the following sentences. Read the sentences and word choices aloud. Have the student choose the word that makes sense in the sentence. Have him or her write the sentences in the journal.
  1. It _____ a hot dog. (is, are)
  2. _____ was Jim's wife. (She, They)

3. Sue planted _____ elm tree.
   (a, an)
4. _____ live on Oak Street.
   (He, They)

• Have the student circle the sight words in the word search below. The words may be written forward, backward, and up and down.

```
a  t  h  e  y  o  u
n  h  a  s  h  e  w
t  i  h  e  d  i  a
h  s  a  r  e  s  s
a  w  u  y  e  h  t
t  t  g  v  m  o  i
```

• Have the student read the following paragraph and underline the new sight words in it. Have him or her answer the questions following the paragraph.

I can use this key to open the door. He and she can use the key to open the door. You can use the key to open the door. They are knocking on the door.

Ask the student: Who can use the key to open the door? (I, He and she, You) Who cannot use the key? (They) What must they do to open the door? (knock)

UNIT 4, LESSON 3

More Practice
Pages 67–71, 81–85, 92–94

I. LESSON OVERVIEW

This lesson provides further practice with sight words studied previously by grouping the words into phrases such as *you are* and *he is*. Use this lesson as a model for all the More Practice pages in Unit Four.

II. STUDENT OUTCOMES

The student will recognize, read, and write sight words in phrases and in new contexts.

III. PROCEDURES

Adapt the procedures in this lesson for page 67 to present all the More Practice pages in Unit Four.

Exercise A. Read the phrases *you are* and *he is,* and *she is* as the student listens. Ask him or her to repeat the phrases. Read each numbered group of sentences aloud, and have the student repeat them. Emphasize that each group of sentences tells a story. Have the student write the practice words on the lines provided. Remind him or her to use a capital letter to begin the word when the practice word in the sentence is capitalized. Have the student reread the sentences and write them in the journal.

Exercise B. Discuss the picture together. Read the two groups of sentences aloud, and have the student repeat them. Remind him or her that only one set of sentences describes the picture. Have the student choose the correct group of sentences and write them.

IV. FOLLOW-UP ACTIVITIES

The following activities are designed to reinforce the student's mastery of sight words in phrases.

• Have the student make flash cards of the practice phrases and then write them in the journal.

• Write the practice phrases incorrectly by reversing the pronouns: *you is* and *he are.* Ask the student what is wrong with these phrases. (Lead him or her to say, "They sound funny" or "The words don't go together.") Then write the phrases correctly. Point out that memorizing the words in phrases is one way of mastering them. You may want to introduce singular and plural pronouns since page 68 teaches *they*. Dictate several phrases (such as *I am, you are, he is, she is, they are*) for the student to repeat and use in sentences.

• Write the following sentences and have the student choose the word in parentheses that completes the sentence. Have him or her write all the sentences in the journal.

1. He _____ happy. (is, are)
2. You _____ sad. (is, are)
3. _____ are learning. (You, He)
4. _____ is learning. (You, He)
5. He _____ reading. (is, are)

6. You _____ reading. (is, are)
7. He _____ going swimming. (is, are)
8. You _____ going swimming. (is, are)
9. You and he _____ going swimming. (is, are)
10. They _____ going swimming. (is, are)

UNIT 4, LESSON 4

Review and Practice
Pages 72–73, 79–80, 86–87, 91 and 95

I.   LESSON OVERVIEW

This lesson reviews and provides further practice with these sight words and phrases: *you are, he is, they are, that is, she and I, this is, it was, a, the, this was,* and *that was.* Use this lesson as a model for teaching the Review and Practice pages in Unit Four.

II.   STUDENT OUTCOMES

The student will recognize, read, and write sight words and phrases in context.

III. PROCEDURES

Adapt the procedures in this lesson to review all the sight words and phrases.
Review, Exercise A. Ask the student to look at each picture on page 72, and then read the sentences aloud using both word choices. Have him or her write the choice that makes better sense in the blank. Discuss why the other choices are incorrect. Have the student write the sentences in the journal.
Exercise B. Read the directions on page 73 together. Have the student read the word choices in each word box and select the one that makes the most sense in each sentence. Have him or her read the completed sentences aloud. Then have the student write the paragraph in the journal.

Exercise C. Read the directions together. Have the student read the words from the word box and the paragraph aloud. Have him or her underline the words from the word box that appear in the paragraph.

IV.   FOLLOW-UP ACTIVITIES

The following activities are designed to reinforce the student's mastery of sight words and phrases.
• Dictate any of the sight words and phrases from pages 60–95. Have the student write them and use each in a sentence.
• Point to an object near you and say, "This is a _____ ." Then point to something farther away and say, "That is a _____ ." Have the student make up other sentences about objects in the room.
• Copy the six sentences below. Read the sentences and word choices and have the student repeat. Then have him or her circle the word or phrase that completes each sentence.
  1. _____ the first day on my new job.
     This is   They are   He is
  2. _____ going on a picnic.
     That is   It was   They are
  3. _____ like to go to the park.
     He and she   That is   He is
  4. _____ ride a bus to the movie.
     She and I   That is   The
  5. You are reading _____ book.
     a   it is   that was
  6. _____ driving 50 miles a day.
     It was   She was   This is
• Copy the paragraph below. Read the paragraph and have the student repeat. Then ask him or her to underline the sight words and phrases reviewed in this lesson. (The answers are in italics.)

   That is the truck *she and I* want to buy.
   It is large. *The* cab is roomy. *The* children are happy. *They are* telling their friends,
   "*This is* our new truck."

UNIT 4, LESSON 5

Number Words
Pages 96–97

I. LESSON OVERVIEW

This lesson introduces the number words *zero, one, two, three, four, five, six, seven, eight, nine,* and *ten*.

II. STUDENT OUTCOMES

The student will recognize, read, and write the number words *zero* through *ten*.

III. PROCEDURES

Repeat the following procedures for page 96 to teach the number words *six, seven, eight, nine,* and *ten* on page 97.

Page 96, Exercise A. Write the number words *zero, one, two, three, four,* and *five,* and read them aloud as the student listens. Then ask him or her to read the word and write the numbers that go with the words. Have the student look at the pictures and read the words and numbers. Then have him or her write the number word under the picture.

Exercise B. Have the student draw lines to match the number with the number word.

Exercise C. Have the student rearrange the order of the number words and write them in order from smallest to largest.

Page 98. When you think the student is ready, have him or her do the review lesson on pages 98–99. Help the student read the story on page 99.

IV. FOLLOW-UP ACTIVITIES

The following activities are designed to reinforce the student's mastery of the number words *zero* through *ten*.

• Have the student make flash cards for the number words and then write the words in the journal.

• Have the student write sentences using the number words *zero* through *ten*. Have him or her write the sentences in the journal.

• Have the student say the numbers *zero, one, two, three, four,* and *five*. Then ask him or her to say them in descending order. Ask the student to recall hearing a countdown such as in space shuttle launches and sports activities.

UNIT 4, LESSON 6

Writing Skills: Writing Numbers
Pages 100–101

I. LESSON OVERVIEW

This lesson gives the student practice identifying number words and introduces ordinals.

II. STUDENT OUTCOMES

The student will recognize, read, and write the number words *one* through *ten* and the ordinals *first* through *tenth*.

III. PROCEDURES

Repeat the following procedures for pages 100–101 to practice the two kinds of number words.

Exercise A. Have the student write the words and circle the pictures.

Exercise B. Have the student look at the pictures and read the sentences. Help the student count the objects in each picture and write the correct number words below it.

UNIT 4, LESSON 7

Final Review
Page 102–104

I. LESSON OVERVIEW

This lesson reviews and assesses the student's grasp of consonant and vowel sounds, the sight words in Book One, the inflectional endings *–s, –es, –ed,* and *–ing,* and number words. Use this lesson as a review or a test.

II. STUDENT OUTCOMES

The student will recognize, read, and write words taught in Book One.

III. PROCEDURES

Exercise A. Read the directions together and then help the student do item 1: *cat, can, cup, cap, cake,* and *cone.* Have him or her complete the exercise. Help as necessary. Check the student's work.

Exercise B. Read the directions together and help the student do item 1: *bin* rhymes with *pin,* for example. Check the student's work.

Exercise C. Read the directions together and help the student do item 1: *bed.* The student may want to look through the book to find the words. Check the student's work.

Exercise D. Read the directions together. Have the student read the sentences and the words in the word boxes and then write the word that makes sense in the sentence. Check the student's work.

Exercise E. Read the directions together. Have the student read the sentences and write the ending on the line. Then have the student write the new word. Check the student's work.

Exercise F. Have the student look at the picture and write the correct number word in each sentence. Check the student's work.

IV. FOLLOW-UP ACTIVITIES

The following activities are designed to reinforce the student's mastery of sight words and letter-sound associations.

• Have students review their deck of flash cards for examples of words with beginning consonant and vowel sounds. Help students recall the key picture for each initial consonant and vowel sound.

• Have the student make up sentences with the first words listed in Exercise C on page 102. Have him or her read the sentences aloud and then write them in the journal.

• Dictate several one-syllable words (such as *dog, jam, men, gas, bed, cup, jeep, home*) and ask the student to identify the initial sound. Then have him or her think of additional words beginning with that sound and write them in

sentences. If the student has difficulty thinking of words, ask him or her to look through the journal for previously-taught words.

UNIT 4, LESSON 7

Read a Story (Comprehension)
Pages 105–106

I. LESSON OVERVIEW

This lesson presents a two-page story containing many of the words in Book One.

II. STUDENT OUTCOMES

The student will read, understand, and summarize the story, and answer questions about the story. The student will apply letter-sound associations for consonants and vowels to decode words in context.

III. PROCEDURES

Read. Ask the student to read the title of the story, look at the photos, and predict what the story might be about. Discuss what clues led to the prediction. Read each paragraph aloud and have the student read it after you. Then ask him or her to summarize the events of the story.

Think About It. Review the question words: *who, where, when,* and *why.* Help students read and answer the questions in their own words. Allow students to look back at the story to locate the facts.

IV. FOLLOW-UP ACTIVITIES

The following activities are designed to reinforce the student's understanding of the story.

• Help the student make up more of the story by asking questions that predict what might happen next: What will Ben do with the money? Will he be successful in the job? How might Pam feel about him? Write the extended story as the student dictates it to you and read it back to the student. Then have him or her practice reading the story aloud.

• Have the student bring in a picture of people involved in some event. Discuss the picture together, and ask the student to tell a story about it including details that answer the questions *who, what, where, when,* and *why.* Write the story and read it back to the student. Have him or her answer the *who, what, where, when,* and *why* questions. Have the student practice reading the story aloud and then write it in the journal.

V. WORKBOOK

Assign Workbook One, Unit 4, pages 30–44.

Book Two

Overview

Book Two, written at the 1.0–2.0 reading level, begins the seven-unit structure of all subsequent books in the *Reading for Today* program. Each unit focuses on a different life-coping theme such as managing money, and integrates a high-interest story with phonics, language, and comprehension questions. The story opener and accompanying photo get students involved in a story that continues on exercise pages in the unit. Students practice reading known sight words and apply basic phonics patterns to phonetically regular words. New sight words are introduced on a controlled basis within the context of the story and are frequently practiced throughout the unit. Students are encouraged to practice sight words and phonics words by keeping a journal of these words, sentences using the words in context, and original sentences and paragraphs.

Writing skills introduced in Book Two provide the student with the basic rules of sentence structure and with word-building exercises designed to reinforce the reading-writing connection. Language experience activities based on the writing skills lesson in each unit continue the writing method practiced in the Introductory Book and Book One.

After completing sight word, phonics, and writing skills exercises, the student reviews the events of the story and the photo to predict what will happen in the rest of the story. Each unit concludes with comprehension questions designed to review key points in the story and to give the student the opportunity to react to the story in discussion or in writing. Students practice the basic reading comprehension skills of summarizing, recalling facts and details, finding the main idea, sequencing events, inferring, drawing conclusions, and determining cause and effect.

Each unit in Book Two contains six kinds of lesson pages:

Unit Opener presents a unit theme, related story title, and photo to stimulate discussion about the story. Students relate their own experiences and predict what they think the story is about.

Review Words reinforces twelve words from a prior unit or book.

Sight Words introduces new words in the context of a sentence.

Phonics teaches short vowel sounds by building a word-family list using consonant substitution.

Writing Skills teaches word-analysis skills such as forming the possessive of known words.

Comprehension concludes the story and allows students to apply all the skills introduced in the unit to answer comprehension questions in discussion or individual writing assignments.

Each unit in the student book has a corresponding Unit Review and Workbook Two unit:

Unit Review reviews the reading skills taught in each unit and can be used after the completion of the unit or of the complete book before moving on to Book Three.

Workbook Two presents new stories related to the unit theme of the student book to extend the phonics and language lessons taught in the student book, provide reinforcement of sight words in context, and practice comprehension and writing skills.

All words introduced in Book Two on sight word, phonics, and language pages are included in the master *Word List* on pages 121–122.

UNIT 1 • (Pages 2-15)

Managing Money: "A Chance to Win"

I.   STORY OVERVIEW

Matt does not have enough money to go see the music group Brother Fox. He thinks he will have to stay home, but he wins a ticket on a radio program. Students discuss managing money and accepting help from others.

II.   OUTCOMES AND PROCEDURES

Unit Opener   Pages 2-3

Student Outcome: The student will apply prior knowledge and predicting skills to a new reading selection.

Procedures

1. Read the unit title and story title to the students or have students read.
2. Read the Discussion questions on page 3 to the students and discuss the title of the story and the characters and situation in the photo. Do not rush this activity.
3. Read the story as the students follow along. Then read it together. Review any words the students do not recognize.
4. Ask students to predict what will happen in the rest of the story.

Review Words   Page 4

Student Outcome: The student will recognize 12 previously-taught sight words: *money, first, bills, cannot, where, fan, very, have, brother, does, their,* and *sit.*

Procedures

1. Listen to students read the review words aloud. Explain that these words were presented in prior units.
2. Have students check known words.
3. Practice reading any words the students do not recognize. Give students a sentence containing each word to reinforce the word's meaning.
4. Read the directions for Exercises A-C to the students. Help students as needed as they work.

Optional Activities

• Dictate the review words to students to write.
• Have students write sentences using the review words.
• Have students classify review words into groups (describing words, naming words, action words, connecting words, words that take the place of naming words).

Sight Words   Pages 5-7

Student Outcome: The student will demonstrate recognition of 9 new sight words: *lucky, wallet, ticket, lose, on, upset, sat, chance, plan.*

Procedures

1. Read each sight word aloud. Have the students repeat.
2. Read the directions for Exercises A-E to the students. Help the students as needed as they work. Check the answers together.

Optional Activities

• Have students write the new words on index cards for flash-card practice. Students can work in pairs or with the instructor. Have them study all nine sight words in Unit 1 using the cards.
• Discuss the difference between action and naming words (or verbs and nouns). Ask students to write the action and naming sight words.
• Homework: Have students start a journal of new sight words. Words can be organized by unit or alphabetically. Have the students practice writing sentences from Review Words and Sight Words.

Phonics   Pages 8-9

Student Outcomes: The student will review the short *a* vowel sound and associate it with the *-at* word family.

Procedures

1. Read the words in color. Discuss how new words are formed in the same word families by combining other consonant sounds with *-at.* Review the basic consonant-short vowel-consonant (CVC) spelling pattern in the words. Make sure students are blending sounds as they read the words.

2. Tell students that the vowel letter *a* on page 8 stands for the short *a* sound in the words *plan, can, fan,* etc. Tell students the vowel letter *a* on page 9 stands for the short *a* sound in *sat, bat, cat,* etc. Have the students write the words that have the CVC spelling pattern in their journals.

3. Read the directions for Exercises A–D to the students. Tell the students that in Exercise C on page 9, the correct answer must make sense with the rest of the sentence (context). Help the students select the correct answer.

Optional Activities
• Have students identify and write the names of objects in the room that have the short *a* sounds that are in the *–an* and *–at* word families. Ask them to make up sentences with the words and write them in their journals.

• Homework: Encourage students to start a vocabulary journal of words from the *–an* and *–at* word families. (For more example words, see the Word List on pages 121–122.)

Writing Skills   Pages 10–11
Student Outcome: The student will capitalize the first words of sentences and use correct end marks.

Procedures
Explain that every sentence begins with a capital letter. Review the end marks: the period, the question mark, and the exclamation point. Read the directions for Exercises A–E to the students.

Optional Activities
• Have students write three sentences using the sight words *lucky, wallet, ticket, lose, on, upset, sat, chance,* and *plan.* Make sure the student capitalizes the first word of each sentence and uses an appropriate end mark.

• Language Experience: Ask the student to tell you a story about managing money. After writing the student's story and having the student read to you, ask him or her to circle all the capital letters and end marks.

Back to the Story   Pages 12–14
Student Outcomes: The student will apply recalling and predicting skills; read new sight words, word family words, and plurals in context.

Procedures
1. Read the question on page 12 to the students. Ask students to review the events of the story thus far. Have students look at the picture and predict what they think will happen in the rest of the story.

2. Read the story on pages 12–14 to the students or have them read. If students read the story and feel comfortable doing so, ask them to take parts (Van, Matt, Gate Man) and read with expression. Review any words the students do not recognize.

3. Point out the different types of punctuation ending sentences in the story: period, question mark, and exclamation point. Explain that periods follow statements, question marks follow questions, and exclamation points follow expressions of emotion. Have the students find examples of each type of punctuation and write the sentence it follows.

Comprehension: Think and Write
Page 14
Student Outcomes: The student will apply basic comprehension skills (main idea, details, sequence, inference, cause and effect, and drawing conclusions) to understanding the story; summarize the events in the story and relate events to the student's own experience.

Procedures
1. Read the questions in Think About It to the students or have them read. Help students answer questions. Review the story if necessary to help students find information to support answers. Give the students ample time to look back at the story and consider their answers.

Ask the additional questions: Why didn't Matt have the money to buy a ticket? What might have happened if Matt had not been the fifth caller? If another band Matt likes comes to town, will he be able to buy a ticket?

2. Ask students to express their opinion when they answer the question in Write About It. Help students with their writing as necessary.

Unit Review   Page 15

Student Outcome: The student will demonstrate mastery of the vocabulary, phonics, and writing skills covered in the unit.

III. WORKBOOK

Assign Workbook Two, Unit 1, pages 3–10.

IV. POST-READING DISCUSSION

• Discuss what else Matt could have done to get money for the ticket. Ask students what they would have done.

• Ask the students if people usually win things they want in contests. Ask them if they have ever won anything they wanted.

• Discuss whether Van should have asked whether he could get in without a ticket. Should the gate man have let him in without paying?

UNIT 2 • *(Pages 16-29)*

Moving to Find Work: "A New Job"

I. STORY OVERVIEW

The main character moves to another part of the city to take a better job. She brings her mother from the country and finds a job for her brother. She brings her mother and brother to live with the family. Students discuss moving to find better job opportunities and solving family problems.

II. OUTCOMES AND PROCEDURES

Unit Opener   Pages 16–17

Student Outcome: The student will apply prior knowledge and predicting skills to a new reading selection.

Procedures
1. Read the unit title and story title to the students or have students read.
2. Read the Discussion questions on page 17 with the students and discuss the title of the story and the characters and situation in the photo. Do not rush this activity.
3. Read the story as the students follow along. Then read it together. Review any words the students do not recognize.
4. Ask students to predict what will happen in the rest of the story.

Review Words   Page 18

Student Outcome: The student will recognize 12 previously-taught sight words: *key, look, family, sister, desk, go, chance, big, brother, pays, home, work.*

Procedures
1. Listen to students read the review words aloud. Explain that these words were presented in prior units.
2. Have students check known words.
3. Practice reading any words the students do not recognize. Give students a sentence containing each word to reinforce the word's meaning.
4. Read the directions for Exercises A–C with the students. Help students as needed as they work.

Optional Activities
• Dictate the review words to students to write.
• Have students write sentences using the review words.
• Have students classify review words into groups (describing words, naming words, action words, connecting words, words that take the place of naming words).

Sight Words   Pages 19–21

Student Outcome: The student will demonstrate recognition of nine new sight words: *my, got, bigger, children, send, mother, went, love, will.*

Procedures

1. Read each sight word aloud. Have the students repeat. Tell students that *my* rhymes with *why* that they have had before.
2. Read the directions for Exercises A–E with the students. Help the students as needed as they work. Check the answers together.

Optional Activities

• Have students write the new words on index cards for flash-card practice. Students can work in pairs or with the instructor. Have them study all nine sight words in Unit 2 using the cards.

• Discuss the difference between statements and questions. Ask students to find examples of statements and questions and write them in their journals.

• Explain that mother is written with a capital *M* if it is used as a name: Mother, will you come to my school play? If a word showing possession *(my, her, his, our, their)* precedes *mother,* it is written with a small *m:* Her mother is a teacher.

• <u>Homework:</u> Have students continue to add new sight words to their journals and practice writing sentences from Review Words and Sight Words.

Phonics   Pages 22–23

Student Outcomes: The student will review the short *e* vowel sound and associate it with the –*end* and –*ent* word families.

Procedures

1. Read the words in color. Point out the sight words the students already know: *went* and *send.* Discuss how new words are formed in the same word families by combining other consonant sounds with –*end* and –*ent.* Review the basic consonant-short vowel-consonant (CVC) spelling pattern in the words. Make sure students are blending sounds as they read the words.
2. Tell students that the vowel letter *e* stands for the short e sound in the words *bend, send, end, rent, went, tent.* Have the students think of other words of the –*end* and –*ent* word families and write them in their journals.

3. Read the directions for Exercises A–D with the students.

Optional Activities

• Have students identify and write the names of action words (verbs) that have the short e sounds that are in the –*end* and –*ent* word families. Ask them to make up sentences with the words and write them in their journals.

• <u>Homework:</u> Encourage students to add words from the –*end* and –*ent* word families to their vocabulary journals. (For more example words, see the Word List on pages 121–122.)

Writing Skills   Pages 24–25

Student Outcome: The student will form new words by adding –*s,* –*ed,* and –*ing* to verbs.

Procedures

1. Have the students recall that adding –*s* or –*es* to a naming word (noun) means that there is more than one, such as *wallet* and *wallets.* Then explain that adding –*s,* –*es,* –*ed* and –*ing* indicates when an action occurs: She helps (now). She helped (before). She is helping (in progress).
2. Tell the students that in Exercise D on page 24, the correct answer must make sense with the rest of the sentence (context).

Optional Activities

• Explain that words can be used in more than one way. For example, the words *walk* and *rent* can be either verbs or nouns. Have the students complete the following sentences by writing the correct form of the word in parentheses:

He _____ (walk) to work.
He takes a _____ (walk).
She _____ (rent) a VCR.
She pays _____ (rent).

Ask the students to say if the word supplied is a noun or a verb.

• <u>Language Experience:</u> Ask the student to tell you a story about looking for a job. After writing the student's story and having the student read to you, ask him or her to circle the verbs with –*s,* –*es,* –*ed,* or –*ing* in the story.

Back to the Story   Pages 26–28

Student Outcomes: The student will apply recalling and predicting skills; read new sight words, word family words, and verb tenses in context.

Procedures

1. Read the questions on page 26 with the students. Ask students to review the events of the story thus far. Have students look at the picture and predict what they think will happen in the rest of the story.
2. Read the story on pages 26–28 with the students or have them read. Review any words the students do not recognize.
3. Point out the verbs that end in *–s, –es, –ed,* or *–ing.* Explain that verb endings tell us when things happen in relation to each other. Have the students determine the time sequence in the story.

Comprehension: Think and Write
Page 28

Student Outcomes: The student will apply basic comprehension skills (main idea, details, sequence, inference, cause and effect, and drawing conclusions) to understanding the story; summarize the events in the story and relate events to the student's own experience.

Procedures

1. Read the questions in Think About It to the students or have them read. Help students answer questions. Review the story if necessary to help students find information to support answers. Give the students ample time to look back at the story and consider their answers.
   Ask the additional questions: What else could the woman have done to get to her job? How would you get to a job far away from your home?
2. Ask students to express their opinion when they answer the question in Write About It. Help students with their writing as necessary.

Unit Review   Page 29

Student Outcome: The student will demonstrate mastery of the vocabulary, phonics, and writing skills covered in the unit.

III. WORKBOOK

Assign Workbook Two, Unit 2, pages 11–18.

IV. POST-READING DISCUSSION

- Ask the students if they would move to another part of town to be close to their workplaces. Discuss methods of transportation, other than private cars, available to the students.
- Ask the students if their households have several generations (grandparents, children, parents, aunts and uncles) living together. Discuss the advantages and disadvantages of such an arrangement.
- Ask the students to discuss what they know about attitudes toward family in different cultures.

UNIT 3 • *(Pages 30-43)*

Maintaining Health: "Can I Stop?"

I. STORY OVERVIEW

The main character, Van, tries to stop smoking with the aid of a stop-smoking group when smoking is no longer allowed at work. Students discuss maintaining health through preventive care and accepting help from others.

II. OUTCOMES AND PROCEDURES
Unit Opener   Pages 30–31

Student Outcome: The student will apply prior knowledge and predicting skills to a new reading selection.

Procedures

1. Read the unit title and story title to the students or have students read.

2. Read the Discussion questions on page 31 to the students and discuss the title of the story and the characters and situation in the photo.

3. Read the story as the students follow along. Then read together. Review any words the students do not recognize.

4. Ask students to predict what will happen in the rest of the story.

Review Words   Page 32

Student Outcome: The student will recognize 12 previously-taught sight words: *chance, have, help, like, lucky, me, of, pay, people, sick, stop, plan.*

Procedures

1. Listen to students read the review words aloud. Explain that these words were presented in prior units.

2. Have students check known words.

3. Practice reading any words the students do not recognize. Give students a sentence containing each word to reinforce the word's meaning.

4. Read the directions for Exercises A–C to the students. Help students as needed as they work.

Optional Activities

• Dictate the review words to students to write.

• Have students write sentences using the review words.

• Have students classify review words into groups (describing words, naming words, action words, connecting words, words that take the place of naming words).

Sight Words   Pages 33–35

Student Outcome: The student will demonstrate recognition of 9 new sight words: *do, smoke, smoking, health, bet, group, feel, bad, out.*

Procedures

1. Read each sight word aloud. Have the students repeat.

2. Read the directions for Exercises A–E to the students. Help the students as needed as they work. Check the answers together.

Optional Activities

• Have students write the new words on index cards for flash-card practice. Students can work in pairs or with the instructor. Have them study all nine sight words in Unit 3 using the cards.

• Discuss the difference between telling and asking sentences (or statements and questions). Ask students to write statements and questions using sight words.

• Homework: Have students continue to add new sight words in their journals and practice writing sentences using the sight words.

Phonics   Pages 36–37

Student Outcomes: The student will review the short *a* vowel sound and associate it with the –*ad* word family; review the short *e* vowel sound and associate it with the –*et* word family.

Procedures

1. Read the words in color. Point out the words students already know: *bad* and *bet*. Discuss how new words are formed in the same word families by combining other consonant sounds with –*ad* and –*et*. Review the basic consonant-short vowel-consonant (CVC) spelling pattern in the words. Make sure students are blending sounds as they read the words.

2. Tell students that the vowel letter *a* on page 36 stands for the short *a* sound in the words *ad, bad, had*, etc. Tell students the vowel letter *e* on page 37 stands for the short *e* sound in *bet, get, let*, etc.

3. Read the directions for Exercises A–D to the students.

Optional Activities

• Have students identify and write the names of objects in the room that have the short *a* and short *e* sounds or that are in the –*ad* and –*et* word families.

- <u>Homework:</u> Encourage students to add words from the *–ad* and *–et* word families to their vocabulary journals. (For more example words, see the Word List on pages 121–122.)

Writing Skills   Pages 38–39

Student Outcome: The student will form common contractions.

Procedures

1. Compare the sentences without contractions to the sentences with contractions. Discuss which sentences sound more like natural language.
2. Explain that *I'm* and *I am* mean the same thing. Show students how the words are combined and apostrophes are used to replace the letters left out to form contractions.

Optional Activities

- Ask students to name other examples of contractions heard in everyday conversation. Discuss how these contractions are formed. Assist students in writing sentences using the new contractions.
- <u>Language Experience:</u> Ask the student to tell you a story about a habit that he or she has tried to break, or how one might stop a bad habit. After writing the student's story and having the student read to you, ask him or her to circle all contractions in the story.

Back to the Story   Pages 40–42

Student Outcomes: The student will apply recalling and predicting skills; read new sight words, word family words, and contractions in context.

Procedures

1. Read the question on page 40 with the students. Ask students to review the events of the story thus far. Have students look at the picture and predict what they think will happen in the rest of the story.

2. Read the story on pages 40–42 with the students or have them read. If students read the story with you or other students, ask them to take parts reading the story. Review any words the students do not recognize.

Comprehension: Think and Write   Page 42

Student Outcomes: The student will apply basic comprehension skills (main idea, details, sequence, inference, cause and effect, and drawing conclusions) to understanding the story; summarize the events in the story and relate events to the student's own experience.

Procedures

1. Read the questions in Think About It to the students or have them read. Help students answer questions. Review the story if necessary to help students find information to support answers.
   Ask the additional question: How does Van feel about his family's opposition to his smoking?
2. Ask students to express their opinion when they answer the question in Write About It. Help students with their writing as necessary.

Unit Review   Page 43

Student Outcome: The student will demonstrate mastery of the vocabulary, phonics, and writing skills covered in the unit.

III. WORKBOOK

Assign Workbook Two, Unit 3, pages 19–26.

IV. POST-READING DISCUSSION

- Discuss where students might see NO SMOKING signs. What do students know about laws limiting smoking in public places? Discuss the rights of smokers and non-smokers.
- Ask students how being part of a weight-loss group or stop-smoking group might help a person reach a goal.

- Not smoking is part of a total health program. What else could people do to stay well? (proper diet, exercise, enough sleep)

UNIT 4 • (Pages 44-57)

Using Leisure Time: "With My Family"

I. STORY OVERVIEW

The family members in the story celebrate a holiday. They share their holiday with a friend who can't be with his family. Students discuss using leisure time, participating in family activities, and dealing with loneliness on holidays.

II. OUTCOMES AND PROCEDURES

Unit Opener   Pages 44–45

Student Outcome: The student will apply prior knowledge and predicting skills to a new reading selection.

Procedures

1. Read the unit title and story title to the students or have students read.
2. Read the Discussion questions on page 45 with the students and discuss the title of the story and the characters and situation in the photo.
3. Read the story as the students follow along. Then read together. Review any words the students do not recognize.
4. Ask students to predict what will happen in the rest of the story.

Review Words   Page 46

Student Outcome: The student will recognize 12 previously-taught sight words: *brother, bigger, children, family, food, mother, sister, table, two, us, was, with.*

Procedures

1. Listen to students read the review words aloud. Explain that these words were presented in prior units.
2. Have students check known words.

3. Practice reading any words the students do not recognize. Give students a sentence containing each word to reinforce the word's meaning.
4. Read the directions for Exercises A–C with the students. Help students as needed as they work.

Optional Activities

• Dictate the review words to students to write.
• Have students write sentences using the review words.
• Have students classify review words into groups (describing words, naming words, action words, connecting words, words that take the place of naming words).

Sight Words   Pages 47–49

Student Outcome: The student will demonstrate recognition of 9 new sight words: *be, our, holiday, talk, eat, some, top, fed, good.*

Procedures

1. Read each sight word aloud. Have the students repeat.
2. Read the directions for Exercises A–E with the students. Help the students as needed as they work. Check the answers together.

Optional Activities

• Have students write the new words on index cards for flash-card practice. Students can work in pairs or with the instructor. Have them study all nine sight words in Unit 4 using the cards.
• Discuss expressions whose meaning cannot be derived from its words (idioms), such as *kick the bucket.* Ask the students to explain the idiom: *Can we top this (holiday)?* Have them look for other examples.
• <u>Homework:</u> Have students continue to add new sight words to their journals and practice writing sentences. Have them start a list of idioms.

Phonics   Pages 50–51

Student Outcomes: The student will review the short *o* vowel sound and associate it with the *–op* word family; review the short *e* vowel sound and associate it with the *–ed* word family.

Procedures

1. Read the words in color. Point out the words students already know from the Sight Words page: *top* and *fed*. Discuss how new words are formed in the same word families by combining other consonant sounds with *-op* and *-ed*. Review the basic consonant-short vowel-consonant (CVC) spelling pattern in the words. Make sure students are blending sounds as they read the words.
2. Tell students that the vowel letter *o* on page 50 stands for the short *o* sound in the words *top, cop, stop*, etc. Tell students the vowel letter *e* on page 51 stands for the short *e* sound in *fed, bed, led*, etc. Have the students write the words that have the CVC spelling pattern in their journals.
3. Read the directions for Exercises A–D with the students.

Optional Activities

• Point out that in *stop* the letters *s* and *t* go together to stand for the beginning sound they hear. Have the students think of other words that begin with *st* and write them in their journals.
• Homework: Encourage students to add words from the *-op* and *-ed* word families to their vocabulary journal. (For more example words, see the Word List on pages 121–122.)

Writing Skills   Pages 52–53

Student Outcome: The student will form the irregular past tense of the words *get, have, run, lose, send, feel, feed,* and *eat.*

Procedures

1. Explain that some verbs do not form the past tense by adding *-ed*. Instead, these verbs change their spelling. Tell the student that the past tense of these verbs must be memorized.
2. Tell the students that in Exercise C on page 52 and Exercise E on page 53, the correct answer must make sense with the rest of the sentence (context).

Optional Activities

• Ask students to find other words that have an irregular past tense. Assist students in writing sentences using the past tense of the words.
• Language Experience: Ask the student to tell you a story about a holiday experience. After writing the student's story and having the student read to you, ask him or her to circle all irregular past tenses in the story.

Back to the Story   Pages 54–56

Student Outcomes: The student will apply recalling and predicting skills; read new sight words, word family words, and contractions in context.

Procedures

1. Read the questions on page 54 with the students. Ask students to review the events of the story thus far. Have students look at the picture and predict what they think will happen in the rest of the story.
2. Read the story on pages 54–56 to the students or have them read. Review any words the students do not recognize.
3. Have the student make flash cards of all irregular past tenses in the story.

Comprehension: Think and Write Page 56

Student Outcomes: The student will apply basic comprehension skills (main idea, details, sequence, inference, cause and effect, and drawing conclusions) to understanding the story; summarize the events in the story and relate events to the student's own experience.

Procedures

1. Read the questions in Think About It to the students or have them read. Help students answer questions. Review the story if necessary to help students find information to support answers.
   Ask the additional questions: What else could a person do if he or she could not be with family on a holiday?

2. Ask students to express their opinion when they answer the question in Write About It. Help students with their writing as necessary.

Unit Review   Page 57

Student Outcome: The student will demonstrate mastery of the vocabulary, phonics, and writing skills covered in the unit.

III. WORKBOOK

Assign Workbook Two, Unit 4, pages 27–34.

IV. POST-READING DISCUSSION

- Have the students name people who may not be able to be with their families during holidays (ill people in hospitals, civil servants, military personnel).
- Ask the students if they have ever spent a holiday alone. How can a person deal with loneliness on holidays?
- Ask the students if they know people who invite persons who are alone to share their holidays.

UNIT 5 • *(Pages 58-71)*

Job Safety: "Take Time to Be Safe"

I.   STORY OVERVIEW

Tad has an accident on the job. He and his coworkers plan a campaign about safety. Students discuss the importance of job safety and encouraging workers to follow safety rules.

II. OUTCOMES AND PROCEDURES

Unit Opener   Pages 58–59

Student Outcome: The student will apply prior knowledge and predicting skills to a new reading selection.

Procedures

1. Read the unit title and story title to the students or have students read.
2. Read the Discussion questions on page 59 with the students and discuss the title of the story and the characters and situation in the photo.

3. Read the story as the students follow along. Then read together. Review any words the students do not recognize.
4. Ask students to predict what will happen in the rest of the story.

Review Words   Page 60

Student Outcome: The student will recognize 12 previously-taught sight words: *feel, won't, group, water, bills, plan, health, do, help, nurse, table, lucky.*

Procedures

1. Listen to students read the review words aloud. Explain that these words were presented in prior units.
2. Have students check known words.
3. Practice reading any words the students do not recognize. Give students a sentence containing each word to reinforce the word's meaning.
4. Read the directions for Exercises A–C with the students. Help students as needed as they work.

Optional Activities

- Dictate the review words to students to write.
- Have students write sentences using the review words.
- Have students classify review words into groups (describing words, naming words, action words, connecting words, words that take the place of naming words).

Sight Words   Pages 61–63

Student Outcome: The student will demonstrate recognition of 9 new sight words: *mistake, hurt, trouble, safety, eye, but, about, glasses, hand.*

Procedures

1. Read each sight word aloud. Have the students repeat.
2. Read the directions for Exercises A–E with the students. Help the students as needed as they work. Check the answers together.

Optional Activities

• Have students write the new words on index cards for flash-card practice. Students can work in pairs or with the instructor. Have them study all nine sight words in Unit 5 using the cards.

• Discuss the difference between action and naming words (or verbs and nouns). Ask students to write a sentence using *trouble* as a verb and a sentence using it as a noun. "May I trouble you for directions?" "Mistakes make trouble for everyone."

• Explain to the students that *but* is a connecting word (conjunction). Remind them that while *and* connects similar ideas, *but* links contrasting ideas. "I follow safety rules on the job, and my coworkers do also." "I follow safety rules on the job, but my coworkers don't."

• Discuss expressions whose meaning cannot be derived from its words (idioms), such as *get a hand* and *hand in hand*. Ask the students to explain these phrases.

• Homework: Have students continue to add new sight words to their journals and practice writing sentences using sight words.

Phonics   Pages 64–65

Student Outcomes: The student will review the short *u* vowel sound and associate it with the *–ut* word family; review the short *a* vowel sound and associate it with the word family *–and*.

Procedures

1. Read the words in color. Point out the words students already know: *but, and, hand.* Discuss how new words are formed in the same word families by combining other consonant sounds with *–ut* and *–and*. Review the basic consonant-short vowel-consonant (CVC) spelling pattern in the words. Make sure students are blending sounds as they read the words.

2. Tell students that the vowel letter *u* on page 64 stands for the short *u* sound in the words *but, cut, rut,* etc. Tell students the vowel

letter *a* on page 65 stands for the short *a* sound in *hand, band, sand,* etc. Have the students think of additional words and write them in their journals.

3. Read the directions for Exercises A–D with the students.

Optional Activities

• Have the students make up sentences with the words from procedure 2 above, and write the sentences in their journals.

• Homework: Encourage students to add words from *–ut* and *–and* word families to their vocabulary journal. (For more example words, see the Word List on pages 121–122.)

Writing Skills   Pages 66–67

Student Outcome: The student will use capital letters for proper names, the first word of a sentence, and the pronoun *I.*

Procedures

1. Write your own name and the student's name. Point out that each name begins with a capital letter. Write the words *bill* and *Bill.* Explain that the first is a statement of money owed and the second is a person's name. Ask the students to identify the one difference in the appearance of the two words.

2. Read directions for Exercises A–F. Tell the students to capitalize only the first letter of each name and the first word of a sentence and the pronoun *I.*

Optional Activities

• Have the students write sentences using their own names and those of friends.

• Have the students unscramble this sentence: sister works Nan My office in an. (My sister Nan works in an office.)

• Language Experience: Ask the student to tell you a story about a time when he or she or a family member was injured on the job. After writing the student's story and having the student read to you, ask him or her to circle all capital letters in the story.

Back to the Story   Pages 68–70

Student Outcomes: The student will apply recalling and predicting skills; read new sight words, word family words, and capital letters in context.

Procedures

1. Read the question on page 68 with the students. Ask students to review the events of the story thus far. Have students look at the picture and predict what they think will happen in the rest of the story.
2. Read the story on pages 68–70 to the students or have them read taking parts and reading with expression. Review any words the students do not recognize.
3. Point out that a comma is used to indicate a noun of address. (You are lucky, Tad.)

Comprehension: Think and Write   Page 70

Student Outcomes: The student will apply basic comprehension skills (main idea, details, sequence, inference, cause and effect, and drawing conclusions) to understanding the story; summarize the events in the story, and relate events to the student's own experience.

Procedures

1. Read the questions in Think About It to the students or have them read. Help students answer questions. Review the story if necessary to help students find information to support answers.
2. Ask students to express their opinion when they answer the question in Write About It. Help students with their writing as necessary.

Unit Review   Page 71

Student Outcome: The student will demonstrate mastery of the vocabulary, phonics, and writing skills covered in the unit.

III.   WORKBOOK

Assign Workbook Two, Unit 5, pages 35–42.

IV.   POST-READING DISCUSSION

- Discuss safety hazards in the workplace. Ask the students what kind of safety procedures they follow on their jobs.
- Ask the students what federal agencies do to ensure safety in the workplace.
- Have the students discuss safety hazards in the home. What can be done to make homes safer?

UNIT 6 • *(Pages 72-85)*

Understanding Self and Others: "Dad, Mitts, and Me"

I.   STORY OVERVIEW

The main character in this story takes care of her sick dad. She can't go out any more because he doesn't like to be alone. She gets a cat to be a friend for her dad.

II.   OUTCOMES AND PROCEDURES

Unit Opener   Pages 72–73

Student Outcome: The student will apply prior knowledge and predicting skills to a new reading selection.

Procedures

1. Read the unit title and story title to the students or have students read.
2. Read the Discussion questions on page 73 with the students and discuss the title of the story and the characters and situation in the photo.
3. Read the story as the students follow along. Then read together. Review any words the students do not recognize.
4. Ask students to predict what will happen in the rest of the story.

Review Words   Page 74

Student Outcome: The student will recognize 12 previously-taught sight words: *bed, go, feels, out, sit, dishes, talk, work, five, well, that, troubles.*

Procedures

1. Listen to students read the review words aloud. Explain that these words were presented in prior units.
2. Have students check known words.
3. Practice reading any words the students do not recognize. Give students a sentence containing each word to reinforce the word's meaning.
4. Read the directions for Exercises A–C with the students. Help students as needed as they work.

Optional Activities

• Dictate the review words to students to write.
• Have students write sentences using the review words.
• Have students classify review words into groups (describing words, naming words, action words, connecting words, words that take the place of naming words).

Sight Words   Pages 75–77

Student Outcome: The student will demonstrate recognition of 9 new sight words: *did, lot, all, kin, old, age, laugh, read, friends.*

Procedures

1. Read each sight word aloud. Have the students repeat.
2. Read the directions for Exercises A–E with the students. Help the students as needed as they work. Check the answers together.

Optional Activities

• Have students write the new words on index cards for flash-card practice. Students can work in pairs or with the instructor. Have them study all nine sight words in Unit 6 using the cards.
• Review the difference between statements and questions (declarative and interrogative sentences). Have the student change the statements in Exercise B on page 75 into questions. (Do my brothers and I love Dad a lot?)
• Point out that friends begins with *fr.* The letters *f* and *r* blend to stand for the sound heard

in *friends, from,* and *fruit.* Ask the students to think of other words that begin with *fr* such as *frog, Friday, free, France.* Have them write sentences in their journals using these *fr* words.
• Homework: Have students continue to add new sight words to their journals and practice writing sentences using sight words.

Phonics   Pages 78–79

Student Outcomes: The student will review the short *i* vowel sound and associate it with the *–in* word family; review the short *o* vowel sound and associate it with the *–ot* word family.

Procedures

1. Read the words in color. Point out the words students already know: *kin* and *lot.* Discuss how new words are formed in the same word families by combining other consonant sounds with *–in* and *–ot.* Review the basic consonant-short vowel-consonant (CVC) spelling pattern in the words. Make sure students are blending sounds as they read the words.
2. Tell students that the vowel letter *i* on page 78 stands for the short *i* sound in the words *kin, pin, tin, win,* etc. Tell students the vowel letter *o* on page 79 stands for the short *o* sound in *lot, cot, dot, hot,* etc. Have the students write in their journals the words that have the CVC spelling pattern.
3. Read the directions for Exercises A–D to the students.

Optional Activities

• Have students identify and write the names of objects that have the short *i* sound that are in the *–in* word family and the short *o* sound in the *–ot* word family. Ask them to make up sentences with the words and write them in their journals.
• Homework: Encourage students to add words from the *–in* and *–ot* word families to their vocabulary journal. (For more example words, see the Word List on pages 121–122.)

Writing Skills   Pages 80–81

Student Outcome: The student will form the singular possessive of nouns by adding *'s.*

Procedures

1. Explain that adding *'s* makes a noun possessive and shows ownership (Lin's car, Joe's shirt, Dad's kin).
2. Tell the students that in Exercise C on page 80 and Exercise E on page 81, the answer must make sense with the rest of the sentence (context).

Optional Activities

• Ask the students to write the *'s* (possessive) forms of each of these phrases:
   a. help of the family (family's help)
   b. old car of Lin (Lin's old car)
   c. work of Jed (Jed's work)
   d. kin of Dad (Dad's kin)
   e. help of the nurse (the nurse's help)
• <u>Language Experience:</u> Ask the student to tell you a story about taking care of someone who was ill. After writing the student's story and having the student read to you, ask him or her to circle all possessive nouns in the story.

Back to the Story   Pages 82–84

Student Outcomes: The student will apply recalling and predicting skills; read new sight words, word family words, and possessive nouns in context.

Procedures

1. Read the questions on page 82 with the students. Ask students to review the events of the story thus far. Have students look at the picture and predict what they think will happen in the rest of the story.
2. Read the story on pages 82–84 to the students or have them read, taking parts and reading with expression. Review any words the students do not recognize.
3. Review the different types of punctuation ending sentences in the story: period, question mark, and exclamation point. Have

the students find examples of each type of punctuation and write the sentence it follows.
4. Explain that a compound sentence has two complete thoughts joined by a conjunction. (It's a light, and you can set it on the stand by the bed.)
Have the students look at the last sentence of the story and decide if it is a compound sentence.

Comprehension: Think and Write Page 84

Student Outcomes: The student will apply basic comprehension skills (main idea, details, sequence, inference, cause and effect, and drawing conclusions) to understanding the story; summarize the events in the story, and relate events to the student's own experience.

Procedures

1. Read the questions in Think About It to the students or have them read. Help students answer questions. Review the story if necessary to help students find information to support answers.
2. Ask students to express their opinion when they answer the question in Write About It. Help students with their writing as necessary.

Unit Review   Page 85

Student Outcome: The student will demonstrate mastery of the vocabulary, phonics, and writing skills covered in the unit.

III.   WORKBOOK

Assign Workbook Two, Unit 6, pages 43–50.

IV.   POST-READING DISCUSSION

• Ask the students what kinds of things a healthy person can do for a sick person.
• Ask the students what a sick person might do to feel less lonely.
• Discuss what community resources are available for people without family to care for them.

UNIT 7 • (Pages 86-99)

Finding a Satisfying Job: "A Chance at the Big Time"

I.   STORY OVERVIEW

The main character tells about his struggle to get his parents to accept and support his career choice—playing with a band. Students discuss finding a satisfying job, communicating between adolescents and parents, and persevering to achieve a goal.

II.   OUTCOMES AND PROCEDURES

Unit Opener   Pages 86–87

Student Outcome: The student will apply prior knowledge and predicting skills to a new reading selection.

Procedures
1. Read the unit title and story title to the students or have students read.
2. Read the Discussion questions on page 87 with the students and discuss the title of the story and the characters and situation in the photo.
3. Read the story as the students follow along. Then read together. Review any words the students do not recognize.
4. Ask students to predict what will happen in the rest of the story.

Review Words   Page 88

Student Outcome: The student will recognize 12 previously-taught sight words: *band, chance, good, group, home, lose, mistake, mother, read, this, plan, trouble.*

Procedures
1. Listen to students read the review words aloud. Explain that these words were presented in prior units.
2. Have students check known words.
3. Practice reading any words the students do not recognize. Give students a sentence containing each word to reinforce the word's meaning.

4. Read the directions for Exercises A–C with the students. Help students as needed as they work.

Optional Activities
• Dictate the review words to students to write.
• Have students write sentences using the review words.
• Have students classify review words into groups (describing words, naming words, action words, connecting words, words that take the place of naming words).

Sight Words Pages 89–91

Student Outcome: The student will demonstrate recognition of 9 new sight words: *guitar, music, fit, son, plays, his, father, find, fun.*

Procedures
1. Read each sight word aloud. Have the students repeat.
2. Read the directions for Exercises A–E with the students. Help the students as needed as they work. Check the answers together.

Optional Activities
• Have students write the new words on index cards for flash-card practice. Students can work in pairs or with the instructor. Have them study all nine sight words in Unit 7 using the cards.
• Review the difference between statements and questions (declarative and interrogative sentences). Ask students to change the declarative sentences in Exercise B on page 89 into interrogative sentences (Did my dad get me the guitar?). If the sentence is already a question, change it to a statement (This guitar can help me get a job in the band).
• Discuss expressions whose meaning cannot be derived from its words (idioms), such as *fit in.* Ask the students to explain the idiom. Have them look for other examples. Have the students write the examples in their journals.
• Homework: Have students continue to add new sight words to their journals and practice writing sentences using sight words.

Phonics   Pages 92–93

Student Outcomes: The student will review the short *u* vowel sound and associate it with the –*un* word family; review the short *i* vowel sound and associate it with the –*it* word family.

Procedures

1. Read the words in color. Point out the words students already know: *fun* and *fit*. Discuss how new words are formed in the same word families by combining other consonant sounds with –*un* and –*it*. Review the basic consonant-short vowel-consonant (CVC) spelling pattern in the words. Make sure students are blending sounds as they read the words.
2. Tell students that the vowel letter *u* on page 92 stands for the short *u* sound in the words *fun, run, sun,* etc. Tell students the vowel letter *i* on page 93 stands for the short *i* sound in *fit, hit, lit,* etc.
3. Read the directions for Exercises A–D with the students.

Optional Activities

• Ask students to make up sentences with other –*un* and –*it* words (*pun, spun, shun, gun, knit, spit, kit, pit*) and write them in their journals.
• Homework: Encourage students to add words from –*un* and –*it* word families to their vocabulary journal. (For more example words, see the Word List on pages 121–122.)

Writing Skills   Pages 94–95

Student Outcome: The student will recognize and write the question words *who, what, where, when, why,* and *how.*

Procedures

1. Explain to students that sentences beginning with the words *who, what, where, when, why,* and *how* are questions.
2. Tell the students that in Exercise C on page 94, the answer must make sense with the rest of the sentence (context).

Optional Activities

• Ask students to find sentences that begin with question words and write them in their journals.
• Write the sentences *Who likes to play music? What band do you like? Where do you hear music? Why do you like music? When will the band play?* and *How does the band sound?* Ask the student to circle the question word in each sentence.
• Language Experience: Ask the student to explain why he or she would or would not want to work in a band that is "on the road" often. Write the student's response and have the student read to you.

Back to the Story   Pages 96–98

Student Outcomes: The student will apply recalling and predicting skills; read new sight words, word family words, and verb tenses in context.

Procedures

1. Read the question on page 96 with the students. Ask students to review the events of the story thus far. Have students look at the picture and predict what they think will happen in the rest of the story.
2. Read the story on pages 96–98 to the students or have them read. Review any words the students do not recognize.

Comprehension: Think and Write Page 98

Student Outcomes: The student will apply basic comprehension skills (main idea, details, sequence, inference, cause and effect, and drawing conclusions) to understanding the story; summarize the events in the story and relate events to the student's own experience.

Procedures

1. Read the questions in Think About It to the students or have them read. Help students answer questions. Review the story if necessary to help students find information to support answers.

2. Ask students to express their opinion when they answer the question in Write About It. Help students with their writing as necessary.

Unit Review   Page 99

Student Outcome: The student will demonstrate mastery of the vocabulary, phonics, and writing skills covered in the unit.

III. WORKBOOK

Assign Workbook Two, Unit 7, pages 51–58.

IV. POST-READING DISCUSSION

- Ask the students if they would want their children to be musicians or artists. How important is liking your work?
- Ask what career the students would pursue if they could do whatever they wanted.
- Discuss the importance of music and other forms of artistic expression in a society.

CONCLUDING THE BOOK

At Your Leisure   Pages 100–101

Student Outcome: The student will read the poem and the related prose passage for enjoyment.

Procedures

1. Have students read the poem and story, or read it with them. Help them with any unfamiliar words. Encourage them to talk about what they have read.

2. Talk about the What About You question together or have students write their answer.

Final Review   Pages 102–105

Student Outcome: The student will demonstrate mastery of the vocabulary, phonics, and writing skills covered in Book Two.

Book Three

Overview

Book Three, written at the 2.0–3.0 reading level, continues the seven-unit structure of the *Reading for Today* program. The lesson plan for Unit 1 is complete, and it is the model for the units that follow. For Units 2–7, refer to Unit 1 where indicated in the lesson plans for those units.

UNIT 1 • (Pages 2-15)

Finding Ways to Increase Income: "A Plan to Save the Store"

I. STORY OVERVIEW

Max's music store is not making enough money. Max's brother Kent helps him make a plan to save the store. The plan works, and Max asks Kent to come work with him.

II. OUTCOMES AND PROCEDURES

Unit Opener   Pages 2–3

Student Outcome: The student will apply prior knowledge and predicting skills to a new reading selection.

Procedures

1. Read the unit title and story title to the students or have students read.
2. Discuss the title of the story and the characters and situations in the photo.
3. Read the story as students follow along. Then read together. Review any words the students do not recognize.
4. Ask students to predict what will happen in the rest of the story.

Review Words   Page 4

Student Outcome: The student will recognize 12 previously-taught sight words: *plan, goods, guitars, quit, lose, old, music, won't, some, time, help, trouble.*

Procedures

1. Listen to students read the review words aloud. Explain that these words were presented in prior units.
2. Have students check known words.
3. Practice reading any words the students do not recognize. Give students a sentence containing each word to reinforce the word's meaning.
4. Read the directions for the exercises with the students. Help students as needed as they work.

Sight Words   Pages 5–7

Student Outcome: The student will demonstrate recognition of 9 new sight words: *see, tapes, sell, take, records, shop, video, down, value.*

Procedures

1. Read each sight word aloud. Have the students repeat.
2. Read the directions for Exercises A–E with the students. Help the students as needed as they work. Check the answers together.
• Review contractions with students. Remind students that the apostrophe in words such as *don't* stands for a missing letter. Have students look for contractions and write them as two separate words *(do not).*
• Review the difference between statements and questions (declarative and interrogative sentences). Ask students to change the declarative sentences in Exercise B on page 5 into interrogative sentences (When people stop by the store, do they see tapes for sale?). Ask students to change the interrogative sentence into a declarative sentence (Max will see that tapes can help the store).

Phonics   Pages 8–9

Student Outcome: Students will review the short *e* and long *a* vowel sounds. They will read and write words with short *e* and long *a* sounds.

Procedures

1. Have students read the words at the top of page 8 and point out that all the words have the short *e* sound. Help students identify the short *e* words in B. Help students as needed with Exercises C and D.

2. Have students read the words at the top of page 9 and point out that all the words have the long *a* sound. Help students identify the long *a* words in B. Help students as needed with Exercises C and D.

Optional Activities

• Have students identify and write the names of objects in the room that have the short *e* or long *a* sounds.

• Homework: Encourage students to add words with the short *e* and long *a* sounds to their vocabulary journals.

Writing Skills: Compound Words
Pages 10–11

• Go over the information in the box with students. Explain that compound words are written without a space between the two parts of the word.

• Help students as needed with Exercises A–F.

Back to the Story   Pages 12–14

Student Outcomes: The student will apply recalling and predicting skills and read new sight words in context.

Procedures

1. Read the questions on page 12 with the students. Ask students to review what they have learned in the story thus far. Have students look at the picture and predict what they think the rest of the story will be about.

2. Read the story on pages 12–14 to the students or have them read. Review any words the students do not recognize.

3. Ask the students the following questions: What did Max do to increase his sales? Why is it important for Max to keep good records for his store?

Comprehension: Think and Write
Page 14

Student Outcomes: The student will apply basic comprehension skills (main idea, details, sequence, inference, cause and effect, and drawing conclusions) to understanding the story; summarize the information in the story and relate ideas to the student's own experience.

Procedures

1. Read the questions in Think About It to the students or have them read. Help students answer questions. Review the story if necessary to help students find information to support answers.

2. Ask students to express their opinion when they answer the question in Write About It. Help students with their writing as necessary.

Unit Review   Page 15

Student Outcome: The student will demonstrate mastery of the vocabulary, phonics, and writing skills covered in the unit.

III. WORKBOOK

Assign Workbook Three, Unit 1, pages 3–10.

UNIT 2 • *(Pages 16-29)*

Rearing Children: "Looking Out for Me"

I.   STORY OVERVIEW

The narrator and her brother Ed were foster children. They found loving foster parents. The narrator lives on her own and hopes to start a family.

II.   OUTCOMES AND PROCEDURES

Unit Opener   Pages 16–17

Follow the outcomes and procedures on page 69 of this guide to teach these pages.

Review Words   Page 18

The 12 previously-taught sight words are: *age, brother, children, father, feel, find, from, laugh, lucky, mother, them, went.*

Follow the outcomes and procedures on page 69 of this guide to teach this page.

Sight Words Pages 19–21
The 9 new sight words are: *parents, who, give, own, fine, life, hug, social worker, when.*
Follow the outcomes and procedures on page 69 of this guide to teach these pages. Adapt the original activities to include:
• Discuss the difference between action and naming words (or verbs and nouns). Ask students to write a sentence using *fine* as a verb and a sentence using it as a noun. "Will the library fine me for the late book?" "I paid my library fine."

Phonics Pages 22–23
Student Outcome: Students will review the short *u* and long *i* vowel sounds. They will read and write words with short *u* and long *i* sounds.
Procedures
1. Have students read the words at the top of page 22 and point out that all the words have the short *u* sound. Help students identify the short *u* words in B. Help students as needed with Exercises C and D.
2. Have students read the words at the top of page 23 and point out that all the words have the long *i* sound. Help students sound out the words in A. Help students identify the long *i* words in B. Help students as needed with Exercises C and D.
Optional Activities
• Have students identify and write the names of objects in the room have short *u* or long *i* sounds.
• Homework: Encourage students to add words that have short *u* or long *i* sounds to their vocabulary journals.

Writing Skills: Irregular Plurals Pages 24–25
• Go over the information in the box with students. Explain that irregular plurals must be memorized.
• Help students as needed with activities A–F.

Back to the Story Pages 26–28
Follow the outcomes and procedures on page 70 of this guide to teach these pages. Adapt the activities to include asking the following additional question: Why did the social worker have to find new homes for the narrator and her brother?

Comprehension: Think and Write Page 28
Follow the outcomes and procedures on page 70 of this guide to teach these pages.

Unit Review Page 29
Student Outcome: The student will demonstrate mastery of the vocabulary, phonics, and writing skills covered in the unit.

III. WORKBOOK
Assign Workbook Three, Unit 2, pages 11–18.

UNIT 3 • *(Pages 30-43)*
Promoting Health Care: "In Good Health"
I. STORY OVERVIEW
The main character is a doctor at a clinic. In her daily log she makes notes about the people who come to the clinic. She works with nurses and social workers to help them.

II. OUTCOMES AND PROCEDURES
Unit Opener Pages 30–31
Follow the outcomes and procedures on page 69 of this guide to teach these pages.

Review Words Page 32
The 12 previously-taught sight words are: *about, but, chance, fine, glasses, group, health, nurse, smoke, smoking, social worker, talk.*
Follow the outcomes and procedures on page 69 of this guide to teach this page.

Sight Words Pages 33–35
The 9 new sight words are: *clinic, hope, doctor, what, problem, said, want, more, hip.*

Follow the outcomes and procedures on page 69 of this guide to teach these pages. Adapt the original activities to include:
• Review the difference between statements and questions (declarative and interrogative sentences). Ask students to change the declarative sentences in Exercise B on page 33 into interrogative sentences (At a good clinic, do all who walk in get help?).

Phonics   Pages 36–37

Student Outcome: Students will review the short *i* and long *o* vowel sounds. They will read and write words with short *i* and long *o* sounds.

Procedures

1. Have students read the words at the top of page 36 and point out that all the words have the short *i* sound. Help students sound out the words in A. Help students identify the short *i* words in B. Help students as needed with Exercises C and D.
2. Have students read the words at the top of page 37 and point out that all the words have the long *o* sound. Help students sound out the words in A. Help students identify the long *o* words in B. Help students as needed with Exercises C and D.

Optional Activities

• Have students identify and write the names of objects in the room have short *i* or long *o* sounds.
• <u>Homework:</u> Encourage students to add words that have short *i* or long *o* sounds to their vocabulary journals.

Writing Skills: Adding *-er* to Naming Words   Pages 38–39

• Go over the information in the box with students. Explain that adding *-er* to words makes them naming words.
• Help students as needed with activities A–F.

Back to the Story   Pages 40–42

Follow the outcomes and procedures on page 70 of this guide to teach these pages. Adapt the activities to include asking the following

additional question: Why does the doctor think Lin H. should get out and see people?

Comprehension: Think and Write Page 42

Follow the outcomes and procedures on page 70 of this guide to teach these pages.

Unit Review   Page 43

Student Outcome: The student will demonstrate mastery of the vocabulary, phonics, and writing skills covered in the unit.

III.   WORKBOOK

Assign Workbook Three, Unit 3, pages 19–26.

UNIT 4 • (Pages 44-57)

Handling Social Relationships: "A Team at Work"

I.   STORY OVERVIEW

Sam and Ray work at Big Value. The new man on their team, Jake, is not pitching in. Sam and Ray talk to their boss about the problem. She tells them how to get Jake on the team.

II.   OUTCOMES AND PROCEDURES

Unit Opener   Pages 44–45

Follow the outcomes and procedures on page 69 of this guide to teach these pages.

Review Words   Page 46

The 12 previously-taught sight words are: *boss, see, hope, helper, trouble, store, problem, takes, hand, asked, lend, work.*
Follow the outcomes and procedures on page 69 of this guide to teach this page.

Sight Words   Pages 47–49

The 9 new sight words are: *need, team, load, day, does, uniform, because, cover, there.*
Follow the outcomes, procedures, and optional activities on page 69 of this guide to teach these pages. Adapt the original activities to include:
• Explain to students that *but* is a connecting word (conjunction). Remind them that while

and connects similar ideas, *but* links contrasting ideas. "We need to work like a team, but Jake will not help us load."

Phonics Pages 50–51
Student Outcome: Students will review the long *a* and long *e* vowel sounds. They will read and write words with long *a* and long *e* sounds.

Procedures
1. Have students read the words at the top of page 50 and point out that all the words have the long *a* sound. Help student sound out the words in A. Help students identify the long *a* words in B. Help students as needed with Exercises C and D.
2. Have students read the words at the top of page 51 and point out that all the words have the long *e* sound. Help students sound out the words in A. Help students identify the *–eed* words in B. Help students as needed with Exercises C and D.

Optional Activities
• Have students identify and write the names of objects in the room have long *a* or long *e* sounds.
• Homework: Encourage students to add words that have long *a* or long *e* sounds to their vocabulary journals.

Writing Skills: Using Commas Pages 52–53
• Go over the information in the box with students. Explain that commas are used to separate parts of a sentence or parts of a date.
• Help students as needed with activities A–D.

Back to the Story Pages 54–56
Follow the outcomes and procedures on page 70 of this guide to teach these pages. Adapt the activities to include asking the following additional question: Why did Jan say Sam and Ray shouldn't get mad and yell at Jake?

Comprehension: Think and Write Page 56
Follow the outcomes and procedures on page 70 of this guide to teach these pages.

Unit Review Page 57
Student Outcome: The student will demonstrate mastery of the vocabulary, phonics, and writing skills covered in the unit.

III. WORKBOOK
Assign Workbook Three, Unit 4, pages 27–34.

UNIT 5 • (Pages 58-71)
Learning About Training Programs: "Helping Dogs to Help People"

I. STORY OVERVIEW
In prison Fay has learned to train dogs to help disabled people. One dog she trained, Sundown, went to a blind woman named June. Fay hopes that she will be able to get a job helping disabled people when she gets out of prison.

II. OUTCOMES AND PROCEDURES
Unit Opener Pages 58–59
Follow the outcomes and procedures on page 69 of this guide to teach these pages.

Review Words Page 60
The 12 previously-taught sight words are: *be, did, do, does, dog, eat, eyes, fed, his, mistake, my, send.* Follow the outcomes and procedures on page 69 of this guide to teach this page.

Sight Words Pages 61–63
The 9 new sight words are: *prison, learn, teach, disabled, different, things, June, come, right.* Follow the outcomes and procedures on page 69 of this guide to teach these pages. Adapt the original activities to include:
• Point out that *things* begins with *th*. The letters *t* and *h* blend to stand for the sound heard in *thin, thank,* and *thorn.* Ask the students to think of other words that begin with *th* such as *theater, thick, thigh, think,* and *third.* Have them write sentences in their journals using these *th* words.

Phonics   Pages 64–65

Student Outcome: Students will review the long *i* and long *u* vowel sounds. They will read and write words with long *i* and long *u* sounds.

Procedures

1. Have students read the words at the top of page 64 and point out that all the words have the long *i* sound. Help students sound out the words in A. Help students identify the long *i* words in B. Help students as needed with Exercises C and D.

2. Have students read the words at the top of page 65 and point out that all the words have the long *u* sound. Help students sound out the words in A. Help students identify the long *u* words in B. Help students as needed with Exercises C and D. Point out to students that the words they circle in Exercise C must make sense in the sentences.

Optional Activities

• Have students identify and write the names of objects in the room that have long *i* or long *u* sounds.

• Homework: Encourage students to add words that have long *i* or long *u* sounds to their vocabulary journals.

Writing Skills: Irregular Verbs
Pages 66–67

• Go over the information in the box with students. Explain that irregular verbs must be memorized.

• Help students as needed with activities A–F.

Back to the Story   Pages 68–70

Follow the outcomes and procedures on page 70 of this guide to teach these pages. Adapt the activities to include asking the following additional question: Why does Fay think teaching dogs to help disabled people is a good thing for a woman in prison to learn?

Comprehension: Think and Write
Page 70

Follow the outcomes and procedures on page 70 of this guide to teach these pages.

Unit Review   Page 71

Student Outcome: The student will demonstrate mastery of the vocabulary, phonics, and writing skills covered in the unit.

III.   WORKBOOK

Assign Workbook Three, Unit 5, pages 35–42.

UNIT 6 • *(Pages 72-85)*

Coping with Job Dissatisfaction: "A Life on the Go"

I.   STORY OVERVIEW

Dell is a trucker. He doesn't like being away from his family, but the pay is good. When the children are older, he will let them stay with his sister and take his wife Hope with him on the road.

II.   OUTCOMES AND PROCEDURES
Unit Opener   Pages 72–73

Follow the outcomes and procedures on page 69 of this guide to teach these pages.

Review Words   Page 74

The 12 previously-taught sight words are: *ads, bet, bigger, fit, hand, holiday, no, on, read, son, upset, will.*
Follow the outcomes and procedures on page 69 of this guide to teach this page.

Sight Words   Pages 75–77

The 9 new sight words are: *drive, rig, road, truck, heavy, carry, cold, lonely, mind.*
Follow the outcomes and procedures on page 69 of this guide to teach these pages. Adapt the original activities to include:

• Discuss expressions whose meaning cannot be derived from their words (idioms), such as *on the road*. Ask the students to explain the idiom. Have them look for another example. Have the students write the idioms in their journals.

Phonics   Pages 78–79

Student Outcome: Students will review the short *i* and long *o* vowel sounds. They will read and write words with short *i* and long *o* sounds.

Procedures

1. Have students read the words at the top of page 78 and point out that all the words have the short *i* sound. Help students sound out the words in A. Help students identify the –*ig* words in B. Help students as needed with Exercises C and D.
2. Have students read the words at the top of page 79 and point out that all the words have the long *o* sound. Help students sound out the words in A. Help students identify the –*old* words in B. Help students as needed with Exercises C and D. Point out to students that the words they circle in Exercise D must make sense in the sentences.

Optional Activities

• Have students identify and write the names of objects in the room have short *i* or long *o* sounds.
• Homework: Encourage students to add words that have short i or long o sounds to their vocabulary journals.

Writing Skills: Dropping Final –*e* To Add –*ed* and –*ing*   Pages 80–81

• Go over the information and examples in the box with students. Explain that because the final –*e* is silent, dropping it does not change the way the word sounds.
• Help students as needed with activities A–F.

Back to the Story   Pages 82–84

Follow the outcomes and procedures on page 70 of this guide to teach these pages. Adapt the activities to include asking the following additional question: Why can't Dell take Hope on the road with him now?

Comprehension: Think and Write Page 84

Follow the outcomes and procedures on page 70 of this guide to teach these pages.

Unit Review   Page 85

Student Outcome: The student will demonstrate mastery of the vocabulary, phonics, and writing skills covered in the unit.

III.   WORKBOOK

Assign Workbook Three, Unit 6, pages 43–50.

UNIT 7 • *(Pages 86-99)*

Working Together for Change: "The Plan That Grew"

I.   STORY OVERVIEW

May, Reed, and Doc are unhappy about a vacant lot in their neighborhood. They make a plan for a garden and ask the city for money. All the neighbors work together to make a wonderful garden.

II.   OUTCOMES AND PROCEDURES

Unit Opener   Pages 86–87

Follow the outcomes and procedures on page 69 of this guide to teach these pages.

Review Words   Page 88

The 12 previously-taught sight words are: *about, children, weeds, hurt, what, someone, play, right, safe, own, there, problem.*
Follow the outcomes and procedures on page 69 of this guide to teach this page.

Sight Words   Pages 89–91

The 10 new sight words are: *camera, still, photo, garden, street, drag, action, many, together, beat.*
Follow the outcomes and procedures on page 69 of this guide to teach these pages. Adapt the original activities to include:
• Review the difference between statements and questions (declarative and interrogative sentences). Ask students to change the declarative sentences in Exercise B on page 89 into interrogative sentences (Will we use this camera to make photo records of the lot?). If the sentence is already a question, change it to a statement (We can still plan a garden where the lot is).

Phonics Pages 92–93

Student Outcome: Students will review the short *a* and long *e* vowel sounds. They will read and write words with short *a* and long *e* sounds.

Procedures
1. Have students read the words at the top of page 92 and point out that all the words have the short *a* sound. Help students sound out the words in A. Help students identify the –*ag* words in B. Help students as needed with Exercises C and D.
2. Have students read the words at the top of page 93 and point out that all the words have the long *e* sound. Help students sound out the words in A. Help students identify the –*eat* words in B. Help students as needed with Exercises C and D. Point out to students that the words they circle in Exercise C must make sense in the sentences.

Optional Activities
• Have students identify and write the names of objects in the room that have short *a* or long *e* sounds.
• Homework: Encourage students to add words that have short *a* or long *e* sounds to their vocabulary journals.

Writing Skills: Quotation Marks Pages 94–95

• Go over the information and examples in the box with students. Explain that it is always important to use quotation marks to show when you are using someone else's exact words.
• Help students as needed with activities A–F.

Back to the Story Pages 96–98

Follow the outcomes and procedures on page 70 of this guide to teach these pages. Adapt the activities to include asking the following additional question: Why did May's group take photos of the old lot?

Comprehension: Think and Write Page 98

Follow the outcomes and procedures on page 70 of this guide to teach these pages.

Unit Review   Page 99

Student Outcome: The student will demonstrate mastery of the vocabulary, phonics, and writing skills covered in the unit.

III. WORKBOOK

Assign Workbook Three, Unit 7, pages 51–58.

CONCLUDING THE BOOK

At Your Leisure Pages 100–101

Student Outcome: The student will read the poem and the related prose passage for enjoyment.

Procedures
1. Have students read the poem and story, or read it with them. Help them with any unfamiliar words. Encourage them to talk about what they have read.
2. Talk about the What About You question together or have students write their answer.

Final Review Pages 102–105

Student Outcome: The student will demonstrate mastery of the vocabulary, phonics, and writing skills covered in Book Three.

Book Four

Overview

Book Four, written at the 3.0–4.0 reading level, continues the seven-unit structure of the *Reading for Today* program. In addition, Book Four introduces two new types of lesson pages, Comprehension Skills and Life Skills. The lesson plan for Unit 1 is complete, and it is the model for the units that follow. For Units 2–7, refer to Unit 1 where indicated in the lesson plans for those units.

UNIT 1 • (Pages 2-17)

Living an Active Life: "One Man, Many Jobs: Ben Nighthorse Campbell"

I. STORY OVERVIEW

This profile of Native American senator Ben Nighthorse Campbell tells about the active life of this remarkable man. The story gives information about his three jobs: being a U.S. senator, running a ranch, and making silver jewelry.

II. OUTCOMES AND PROCEDURES

Unit Opener   Pages 2–3

Student Outcome: The student will apply prior knowledge and predicting skills to a new reading selection.

Procedures

1. Read the unit title and story title with the students.
2. Read the Discussion questions on page 3 with the students and discuss the title of the story and the characters and situations in the photo.
3. Have students read the beginning of the story. Review any words the students do not recognize.
4. Ask students to predict what will happen in the rest of the story.

Review Words   Page 4

Student Outcome: The student will recognize 12 previously-taught sight words: *still, because, hold, many, working, people, together, different, does, action, child, more.*

Procedures

1. Listen to students read the review words aloud. Explain that these words were presented in prior units.
2. Have students check known words.
3. Practice reading any words the students do not recognize. Give students a sentence containing each word to reinforce the word's meaning.
4. Read the directions for the exercises with the students. Help students as needed as they work.

Sight Words   Pages 5–7

Student Outcome: The student will demonstrate recognition of 12 new sight words: *law, been, Native American, here, elected, senator, horse, ranch, put, silver, jewelry, again.*

Procedures

1. Have students read each sight word aloud.
2. Read the directions for Exercises A–D with the students. Help the students as needed as they work. Check the answers together.
• Discuss expressions whose meaning cannot be derived from its words (idioms), such as *put (something) on hold.* Ask the students to explain the idiom. Have them look for other examples. Have the listeners write the examples in their journals.
• Review the difference between statements and questions (declarative and interrogative sentences). Ask students to change the declarative sentences in Exercise B on page 5 into interrogative sentences (Is Ben Nighthorse Campbell a Native American?).

Phonics   Pages 8–9

Student Outcome: The student will review one, two, and three-syllable words and identify the schwa vowel sound.

Procedures

1. Have students read the words in Exercise A on page 8 and point out that every syllable has a vowel and that each syllable may have

one or more consonants. Help students identify the syllables in Exercises B and C.

2. Have students read the words in Exercises A and C on page 9 and identify the schwa sound represented by each of the vowel letters. Help students identify the syllables in Exercise C and the schwa sound in Exercise D.

Optional Activities
• Have students identify and write the names of objects in the room that have more than one syllable or that have the schwa sound.
• Homework: Encourage students to add words with the schwa sound to their vocabulary journals.

Back to the Story   Pages 10–12
Student Outcomes: The student will apply recalling and predicting skills and read new sight words in context.

Procedures
1. Read the question on page 10 with the students. Ask students to review what they have learned in the story thus far. Have students look at the picture and predict what they think the rest of the story will be about.
2. Read the story on pages 10–12 to the students or have them read. Review any words the students do not recognize.
3. Ask the students the following questions: Do you think Ben Nighthorse Campbell is like most other senators? Why or why not?

Comprehension: Think and Write Page 12
Student Outcomes: The student will apply basic comprehension skills (main idea, details, sequence, inference, cause and effect, and drawing conclusions) to understanding the story; summarize the information in the story, and relate ideas to the student's own experience.

Procedures
1. Read the questions in Think About It with the students or have them read. Help students answer questions. Review the story

if necessary to help students find information to support answers.
2. Ask students to express their opinion when they answer the question in Write About It. Help students with their writing as necessary.

Comprehension Skills: Cause and Effect Page 13
• Go over the information and examples in the box with students. Explain that an effect is the result of something that happened and that the cause is the thing that happened. Point out that the cause words and the effect words are sometimes, but not always, used to signal cause and effect.

Writing Skills: Suffixes –*ly* and –*y* Pages 14–15
• Go over the information in the box with students. Explain that words with the suffix –*ly* tell about action words, and words with the suffix –*y* tell about naming words.

Life Skill: Writing a Letter   Page 16
• Ask students to define the words [at the top of the page.] Define any words they don't know for them. Ask students to identify the five parts of the letter in Exercise A. Help them as needed.

Unit Review   Page 17
Student Outcome: The student will demonstrate mastery of the vocabulary, phonics, and writing skills covered in the unit.

III.   WORKBOOK
Assign Workbook Four, Unit 1, pages 3–10.

UNIT 2 • *(Pages 18-33)*

Using Coupons Effectively: "Do You Need to Buy It?"

I.   STORY OVERVIEW
Kay and Nan use coupons at the grocery store to save money, but they buy things they don't need. They use coupons to buy fifty packages of

hot dogs so they can win baseball tickets. Instead, Kay and Nan win more hot dogs.

II. OUTCOMES AND PROCEDURES

Unit Opener   Pages 18–19
Follow the outcomes and procedures on page 77 of this guide to teach these pages.

Review Words   Page 20
The 12 previously-taught sight words are: *baseball, game, thing, because, many, need, buyer, sell, seven, these, see, want.*
Follow the outcome, procedures, and optional activities on page 77 of this guide to teach this page.

Sight Words   Pages 21–23
The 12 new sight words are: *could, coupon, then, save, much, less, think, cost, why, roommate, spend, too.*
Follow the outcomes and procedures on page 77 of this guide to teach these pages. Adapt the original activities to include:
• Review contractions with students. Remind students that the apostrophe in words such as *don't* stands for a missing letter. Have students look for contractions and write them as two separate words (do not).

Phonics   Pages 24–25
Student Outcome: The student will review and identify words that begin with an *r* blend and words that end in *–y* and *–ink.*

Procedures
1. Have students read the words in Exercise A on page 24 and point out that every word begins with an *r* blend sound. Help students identify the letters that stand for *r* blends in Exercises B and C. Point out to students that the words in Exercise C must make sense in the sentence.
2. Have students read the words in Exercises A and C on page 25. Help students sound out the words as needed. Remind students that the words in Exercises B and D must make sense in the sentences.

Optional Activities
• Have students identify and write the names of objects in the room that begin with an *r* blend or end with *–y* or *–ink.*
• <u>Homework:</u> Encourage students to add words that begin with *r* blends or end with *–y* or *–ink* to their vocabulary journals.

Back to the Story   Pages 26–28
Follow the outcomes and procedures on page 78 of this guide to teach these pages. Adapt the activities to include asking the following additional question: Why didn't Nan want Kay to use the coupon for figs?

Comprehension: Think and Write Page 28
Follow the outcomes and procedures on page 78 of this guide to teach these pages.

Comprehension Skills: Inference Page 29
• Go over the information and examples in the box with students. Explain that you make inferences by guessing how two or more facts might go together.

Writing Skills: Irregular Verbs Pages 30–31
• Go over the information in the box with students. Explain that irregular verbs must be memorized.

Life Skill: Reading Coupons Page 32
• Ask students to define the words at the top of the page. Define any words they don't remember. Ask students to find the savings amounts and expiration dates on the coupons. Help them as needed.

Unit Review   Page 33
Student Outcome: The student will demonstrate mastery of the vocabulary, phonics, and writing skills covered in the unit.

III. WORKBOOK
Assign Workbook Four, Unit 2, pages 11–18.

UNIT 3 • (Pages 34-49)

Helping Children Learn to Read: "Who Needs to Read?"

I. STORY OVERVIEW

Mr. Sanders has never learned to read. Now his son is having trouble in school because he doesn't read well. Mr. Sanders decides to learn to read with his son.

II. OUTCOMES AND PROCEDURES

Unit Opener   Pages 34-35

Follow the outcomes and procedures on page 77 of this guide to teach these pages.

Review Words   Page 36

The 12 previously-taught sight words are: *upset, teach, gave, together, learn, said, someone, take, down, teacher, into, who.*
Follow the outcome, procedures, and optional activities on page 77 of this guide to teach this page.

Sight Words   Pages 37-39

The 12 new sight words are: *mean, must, always, school, where, meet, soon, after, or, grade, report, card.*
Follow the outcomes, procedures, and optional activities on page 77 of this guide to teach these pages. Adapt the original activities to include:
• Review possessive words with students. Remind them that most words add *'s* to form the possessive (son's). Have students look for another example.

Phonics   Pages 40-41

Student Outcome: The student will review and identify words that begin with an *s* blend and words that end in *–eet* and *–ean.*

Procedures
1. Have students read the words in Exercise A on page 40 and point out that every word begins with an s blend sound. Help students identify the letters that stand for *s* blends in Exercises B and C. Point out to students that

the words in Exercise C must make sense in the sentence.
2. Have students read the words in Exercises A and C on page 41. Help students sound out the words as needed. Remind students that the words in Exercises B and D must make sense in the sentences.

Optional Activities
• Have students identify and write the names of objects or people in the room whose names begin with an *s* blend or end with *–eet* or *–ean.*
• Homework: Encourage students to add words that begin with *s* blends or end with *–eet* or *–ean* to their vocabulary journals.

Back to the Story   Pages 42-44

Follow the outcomes and procedures on page 78 of this guide to teach these pages. Adapt the activities to include asking the following additional question: Why didn't Jay think it was important to learn to read?

Comprehension: Think and Write Page 44

Follow the outcomes and procedures on page 78 of this guide to teach these pages.

Comprehension Skills: Stated Main Idea Page 45

• Go over the information and examples in the box with students. Explain that the main idea is the idea that the rest of the story tells about. Point out that sometimes the main idea is not in the first paragraph. Then students should look in the second paragraph.

Writing Skills: Prefixes *re–* and *un–* Pages 46-47

• Go over the information in the box with students. Point out that some words start with *re–* and *un–*, such as *read* and *until.* Students should be careful not to confuse the first letters of these words with prefixes.

Life Skill: Reading a Report Card
Page 48

• Ask students to define the words at the top of the page. Define any words they don't remember. Ask students to find the subjects and grades on the report card. Help them as needed.

Unit Review   Page 49

Student Outcome: The student will demonstrate mastery of the vocabulary, phonics, and writing skills covered in the unit.

III. WORKBOOK

Assign Workbook Four, Unit 3, pages 19–26.

UNIT 4 • (Pages 50-65)

Becoming a Parent: "A Family Man"

I. STORY OVERVIEW

Carlos's wife Maria is pregnant. Carlos is excited and they plan carefully for their baby. Finally, the big day comes and Carlos takes Maria to the clinic.

II. OUTCOMES AND PROCEDURES
Unit Opener   Pages 50–51

Follow the outcomes and procedures on page 77 of this guide to teach these pages.

Review Words   Page 52

The 12 previously-taught sight words are: *child, come, clinic, doctor, hope, smoker, drive, hug, parents, heavy, up, street.*
Follow the outcome, procedures, and optional activities on page 77 of this guide to teach this page.

Sight Words   Pages 53–55

The 12 new sight words are: *as, responsible, wife, baby, before, new, know, small, pregnant, tired, rock, late.*
Follow the outcomes, procedures, and optional activities on page 77 of this guide to teach these pages. Adapt the original activities to include:
• Review the difference between statements and questions (declarative and interrogative sentences). Ask students to change the declarative sentences in Exercise B on page 53 into interrogative sentences (Is my wife Maria doing what the doctor told her?).

Phonics   Pages 56–57

Student Outcome: The student will review and identify words that begin with an *l* blend and words that end in *–ock* and *–ate.*

Procedures

1. Have students read the words in Exercise A on page 56 and point out that every word begins with an *l* blend sound. Help students identify the letters that stand for *l* blends in Exercises B and C. Point out to students that the words in Exercise C must make sense in the sentence.
2. Have students read the words in Exercises A and C on page 57. Help students sound out the words as needed. Remind students that the words in Exercises B and D must make sense in the sentences.

Optional Activities

• Have students identify and write the names of objects or people in the room whose names begin with an *l* blend or end with *–ock* or *–ate.*
• Homework: Encourage students to add words that begin with *l* blends or end with *–ock* or *–ate* to their vocabulary journals.

Back to the Story   Pages 58–60

Follow the outcomes and procedures on page 78 of this guide to teach these pages. Adapt the activities to include asking the following additional question: Why does Maria say that having a small child won't be all fun?

Comprehension: Think and Write
Page 60

Follow the outcomes and procedures on page 78 of this guide to teach these pages.

Comprehension Skills:
Implied Main Idea   Page 61

• Go over the information in the box with students. Tell students that to find an implied main idea, they should ask themselves what all the sentences are about. Then they should read the passage again to make sure the main idea makes sense.

Writing Skills: Adding –*ies* or –*s* to Words Ending in –*y*   Pages 62–63
• Go over the information in the box with students. Point out that changing the *y* to *i* does not change the sound of the word because in these words *y* and *i* sound the same.

Life Skill: Reading a Prescription Page 64
• Ask students to define the words at the top of the page. Define any words they don't remember. Ask students to find the directions, quantity, and refill information on the prescription. Help them as needed.

Unit Review   Page 65
Student Outcome: The student will demonstrate mastery of the vocabulary, phonics, and writing skills covered in the unit.

III. WORKBOOK
Assign Workbook Four, Unit 4, pages 27–34.

UNIT 5 • (Pages 66-81)

Understanding Others: "Getting to Know You"

I. STORY OVERVIEW
The Bakers find a strange family near their picnic table. At first Jack Baker is mad about the new family, but when the father helps one of the Baker's children, they make friends.

II. OUTCOMES AND PROCEDURES
Unit Opener   Pages 66–67
Follow the outcomes and procedures on page 77 of this guide to teach these pages.

Review Words   Page 68
The 12 previously-taught sight words are: *bag, player, food, truck, same, him, took, Kate, different, camera, tape, day.*

Follow the outcomes and procedures on page 77 of this guide to teach this page.

Sight Words   Pages 69–71
The 12 new sight words are: *summer, saw, foreign, around, thank, park, snacks, picnic, newcomers, language, grass, jump.*
Follow the outcomes and procedures on page 77 of this guide to teach these pages. Adapt the original activities to include:
• Review the difference between statements and questions (declarative and interrogative sentences). Ask students to change the first declarative sentence in Exercise B on page 69 into an interrogative sentence (Did some friends of mine go to a foreign country this summer?). Then ask students to change the interrogative sentence in Exercise C into a declarative sentence (You have been to a foreign country).

Phonics   Pages 72–73
Student Outcome: The student will review and identify words that begin with consonant digraphs and words that end in –*ack* and –*ank.*

Procedures
1. Have students read the words in Exercise A on page 72 and point out that every word begins with a consonant digraph. Help students identify the consonant digraphs in Exercises B and C. Point out to students that the words in Exercise C must make sense in the sentences.
2. Have students read the words in Exercises A and C on page 73. Help students sound out the words as needed. Remind students that the words in Exercises B and D must make sense in the sentences.

Optional Activities
• Have students identify and write the names of objects or people in the room whose names begin with a consonant digraph or end with –*ack* or –*ank.*
• Homework: Encourage students to add words that begin with consonant digraphs or end with –*ack* or –*ank* to their vocabulary journals.

Back to the Story   Pages 74–76

Follow the outcomes and procedures on page 78 of this guide to teach these pages. Adapt the activities to include asking the following additional question: How did Jack know the new family was not from this country?

Comprehension: Think and Write   Page 76

Follow the outcomes and procedures on page 78 of this guide to teach these pages.

Comprehension Skills: Sequence   Page 77

• Go over the information in the box with students. Explain to students that most stories tell the events in the order in which they happened. If an event is not told in the order in which it happened, it is usually introduced with a time word.

Writing Skills: Suffixes –*ful* and –*ness*   Pages 78–79

• Go over the information and examples in the box with students. Point out that words with the suffix –*ful* can be used to describe things and people. Words with the suffix –*ness* must be used as naming words.

Life Skill: Reading Park Rules   Page 80

• Ask students to define the words in Exercise A. Define any words they don't remember. Ask students to read the rules. Help them as needed.

Unit Review   Page 81

Student Outcome: The student will demonstrate mastery of the vocabulary, phonics, and writing skills covered in the unit.

III.   WORKBOOK

Assign Workbook Four, Unit 5, pages 35–42.

UNIT 6 • *(Pages 82-97)*

Overcoming Shyness: "Lonely in a Group"

I.   STORY OVERVIEW

Rick feels shy at parties. He talks to his friend, Fran, about his problem. Fran gives Rick some tips to overcome his shyness.

II.   OUTCOMES AND PROCEDURES

Unit Opener   Pages 82–83

Follow the outcomes and procedures on page 77 of this guide to teach these pages.

Review Words   Page 84

The 12 previously-taught sight words are: *road, sometimes, fine, give, lonely, own, wife, problem, carry, does, talker, person.*
Follow the outcomes and procedures on page 77 of this guide to teach this page.

Sight Words   Pages 85–87

The 12 new sight words are: *ask, over, would, better, bring, every, party, never, join, company, belong, club.*
Follow the outcomes and procedures on page 77 of this guide to teach these pages. Adapt the original activities to include:
• Discuss expressions whose meaning cannot be derived from its words (idioms) such as *get over (something)*. Ask the students to explain the idiom. Have them look for other examples. Have the students write the examples in their journals.

Phonics   Pages 88–89

Student Outcome: The student will review and identify words with silent letters and words that end in –*ing* and –*ub*.

Procedures

1. Have students read the words in Exercise A on page 88 and point out that every word has silent letters. Help students identify the silent letters in Exercises B and C. Point out

to students that the words in Exercise C must make sense in the sentence.

2. Have students read the words in Exercises A and C on page 89. Help students sound out the words as needed. Remind students that the words in Exercises B and D must make sense in the sentence.

Optional Activities
• Have students identify and write the names of objects or people in the room whose names have silent letters or end with –*ing* or –*ub*.
• Homework: Encourage students to add words that have silent letters or end with –*ing* or –*ub* to their vocabulary journals.

Back to the Story   Pages 90–92
Follow the outcomes and procedures on page 78 of this guide to teach these pages. Adapt the activities to include asking the following additional question: Why can't Rick's wife understand his shyness?

Comprehension: Think and Write Page 92
Follow the outcomes and procedures on page 78 of this guide to teach these pages.

Comprehension Skills: Context   Page 93
• Go over the information in the box with students. Explain that the meanings of unfamiliar words are often given in the sentence before or after the word.

Writing Skills: Abbreviations and Titles Pages 94–95
• Go over the information and examples in the box with students. Explain that people abbreviate common words to save time when writing. Tell students it is important to memorize abbreviations.

Life Skill: Coping with Shyness   Page 96
• Ask students to define the words at the top of the page. Define any words they don't remember. Ask students to read the tips. Help them as needed.

Unit Review   Page 97
Student Outcome: The student will demonstrate mastery of the vocabulary, phonics, and writing skills covered in the unit.

III.   WORKBOOK
Assign Workbook Four, Unit 6, pages 43–50.

UNIT 7 • (Pages 98-113)
Working Toward a Goal: "No Problem with Problems"

I.   STORY OVERVIEW
Jean is applying for a job. While she and her friends are skating, they find an old table. It is too heavy to carry, but Jean puts her skates on the legs and they take it to her friend's home. At her interview she tells how she solved the problem of the table. She gets the job.

II.   OUTCOMES AND PROCEDURES
Unit Opener   Pages 98–99
Follow the outcomes and procedures on page 77 of this guide to teach these pages.

Review Words   Page 100
The 12 previously-taught sight words are: *join, responsible, right, company, about, list, learn, new, problems, when, want, should.*
Follow the outcomes and procedures on page 77 of this guide to teach this page.

Sight Words   Pages 101–103
The 12 new sight words are: *now, center, keep, year, once, listen, solve, interview, straight, career, careful, customers.*
Follow the outcomes, procedures, and optional activities on page 77 of this guide to teach these pages. Adapt the original activities to include:
• Review the difference between statements and questions (declarative and interrogative sentences). Ask students to change the interrogative sentences in Exercise A on page 102 into declarative sentences (You listen well).

Phonics   Pages 104–105

Student Outcome: The student will review and identify words with *y* as a vowel and words that end in *–eep* and *–ear*.

Procedures

1. Have students read the words in Exercise A on page 104 and point out that every word has *y* as a vowel. Help students identify which *y* vowels in the words in Exercises B and C are long *i* and which are long *e*.
2. Have students read the words in Exercises A and C on page 105. Help students sound out the words as needed. Remind students that the words in Exercises B and D must make sense in the sentences.

Optional Activities

• Have students identify and write the names of objects or people in the room whose names have *y* as a vowel or end with *–eep* or *–ear*.
• <u>Homework:</u> Encourage students to add words that have y as a vowel or end with *–eep* or *–ear* to their vocabulary journals.

Back to the Story   Pages 106–108

Follow the outcomes and procedures on page 78 of this guide to teach these pages. Adapt the activities to include asking the following additional question: Why does Jean think she is right for the job of jewelry buyer?

Comprehension: Think and Write Page 108

Follow the outcomes and procedures on page 78 of this guide to teach these pages.

Comprehension Skills: Drawing Conclusions   Page 109

• Go over the information in the box with students. Tell students they should test their conclusions by making sure that they are supported by all the facts.

Writing Skills: Days and Months Pages 110–111

• Go over the information and examples in the box with students. Tell students that they must memorize the abbreviations for the days and months.

Life Skill: Reading a Schedule   Page 112

• Ask students to define the words at the top of the page. Define any words they don't know. Ask students to identify the rows and columns of the table (the rows are for employees, and the columns are for times of the day).

Unit Review   Page 113

Student Outcome: The student will demonstrate mastery of the vocabulary, phonics, and writing skills covered in the unit.

III.   WORKBOOK

Assign Workbook Four, Unit 7, pages 51–58.

CONCLUDING THE BOOK

Final Review   Pages 114–117

Student Outcome: The student will demonstrate mastery of the vocabulary, phonics, and writing skills covered in Book Four.

At Your Leisure   Pages 118–119

Student Outcome: The student will read the poem and the related prose passage for enjoyment.

Procedures

1. Have students read the poem and story, or read it with them. Help them with any unfamiliar words. Encourage them to talk about what they have read.
2. Talk about the What About You question together or have students write their answer.

Book Five

Overview

Book Five, written at the 4.0–5.0 reading level, continues the seven-unit structure of the *Reading for Today* program. The lesson plan for Unit 1 is complete, and it is the model for the units that follow. For Units 2–7, refer to Unit 1 where indicated in the lesson plans for those units.

UNIT 1 • (Pages 2-17)

Finding Work: "You Never Know"

I. STORY OVERVIEW

April is let go from her cleaning job. While she is looking for work, she decides to paint her home. She does a good job, and April finds a job as a painter.

II. OUTCOMES AND PROCEDURES

Unit Opener   Pages 2–3

Student Outcome: The student will apply prior knowledge and predicting skills to a new reading selection.

Procedures
1. Read the unit title and the Discussion box with students. Discuss the story title and the photo.
2. Have students read the beginning of the story and predict what will happen in the rest of the story.

Review Words   Page 4

Student Outcome: The student will recognize 12 previously-taught sight words: *because, how, company, her, around, days, after, other, responsible, find, family, new.*

Procedures
1. Listen to students read the review words aloud. Explain that these words were presented in prior units.
2. Have students check known words.
3. Practice reading any words the students do not recognize. Give students a sentence containing each word to reinforce the word's meaning.

4. Read the directions for the exercises with the students. Help students as needed as they work.

Sight Words   Pages 5–7

Student Outcome: The student will demonstrate recognition of 12 new sight words: *decided, fast, possible, business, worn, walls, marks, paint, done, building, color, under.*

Procedures
1. Read each sight word aloud. Have the students repeat.
2. Read the directions for Exercises A–D with students. Help the students as needed as they work. Check the answers together.
• Explain that quotation marks are used when telling what a person said. Point out the quotations in Exercise D on page 5. Explain to students that when they use quotation marks they must tell who said the words.
• Review the difference between statements and questions (declarative and interrogative sentences). Ask students to change the declarative sentence in Exercise B on page 5 into an interrogative sentence (Did April decide to find out?). Then ask them to change the interrogative sentences to declarative sentences (April could find work in the same business).

Phonics   Pages 8–9

Student Outcome: The student will read and write words from the *–ark* and *–orn* word families and identify and read words with vowels followed by *r*.

Procedures
1. Have students read the words in Exercises A and C on page 8 and point out the basic consonant-vowel-consonant (CVC) pattern. For Exercise D, remind students that the words they write must make sense in the sentences.
2. Have students read the words in Exercise A on page 9 and identify the vowel + *r* sound in each word. For Exercise C, remind students that the words they write must make sense in the sentences.

Optional Activities

• Have students identify and write the names of objects in the room that have vowel + *r* sounds.

• <u>Homework:</u> Encourage students to add words with vowel + *r* sounds to their vocabulary journals.

Back to the Story   Pages 10–12

Student Outcomes: The student will apply recalling and predicting skills and read new sight words in context.

Procedures

1. Read the question in the box with students. Ask students to review what they have learned in the story thus far. Have students look at the picture and predict what they think the rest of the story will be about.

2. Have students read the story on pages 10–12. Review any words the students do not recognize.

3. Ask the students the following questions: Do you think April will succeed at her new job? Why or why not?

Comprehension: Think and Write Page 12

Student Outcomes: The student will apply basic comprehension skills (main idea, details, sequence, inference, cause and effect, and drawing conclusions) to understanding and summarizing, and will use the writing process to relate ideas in the story to the student's own experience.

Procedures

1. Read the questions in Think About It to the students or have them read. Help students answer the questions. Review the story if necessary to help students find information to support answers.

2. Ask students to use their own experiences and opinions when they answer the question in Write About It. Talk about students' ideas with them before they write or have them talk with each other. Help students with their writing as necessary.

Comprehension Skills: Fact and Opinion   Page 13

• Go over the information and examples in the box with students. Explain that opinions are not always signaled by word clues. Sometimes they are stated like facts. To find out if a sentence is a fact or opinion, read the sentence. If you can find out whether it is true or not, it is a fact. If you can't, it is an opinion.

Writing Skills: Subject-Verb Agreement Pages 14–15

• Go over the information in the box with students. Explain that sentences with a subject and verb that don't agree are confusing. Tell students that sentences with two subjects take a plural verb.

Life Skill: Reading Help Wanted Ads Page 16

• Ask students to define the words in Exercise A. Define any words they don't know. Have students read the ads.

Unit Review   Page 17

Student Outcome: The student will demonstrate mastery of the vocabulary, phonics, and writing skills covered in the unit.

III. WORKBOOK

Assign Workbook Five, Unit 1, pages 3–10.

UNIT 2 • *(Pages 18-33)*

Buying Goods on Credit: "Buying on Time"

I.   STORY OVERVIEW

Star and Ray Pope want to buy a new bedroom set, but they don't have much money and they are expecting a baby. They decide to buy the furniture on time. At one store they cannot get the salesman to tell them how much interest they will pay, so they leave. Star and Ray buy a bedroom set at a store with a good name.

II. OUTCOMES AND PROCEDURES

Unit Opener   Pages 18–19
Follow the outcomes and procedures on page 86 of this guide to teach these pages.

Review Words   Page 20
The 12 previously-taught sight words are: *save, spend, pregnant, cost, table, company, wife, bring, straight, baby, coupons, customer.* Follow the outcomes and procedures on page 86 of this guide to teach this page.

Sight Words   Pages 21–23
The 12 new sight words are: *afford, furniture, so, little, pretty, credit, check, name, month, yes, plain, interest.*
Follow the outcomes, procedures, and optional activities on page 86 of this guide to teach these pages. Adapt the original activities to include:
• Discuss expressions whose meaning cannot be derived from its words (idioms), such as *a good name.* Ask the students to explain the idiom. Have them look for another example. Have the students write the idioms in their journals.

Phonics   Pages 24–25
Student Outcome: The student will read and write words that end in *–ain* and *–ame* and words with the long *a* sound.

Procedures
1. Have students read the words in Exercises A and C on page 24. Help students sound out the words as needed. Point out to students that the words in Exercises B and D must make sense in the sentences.
2. Have students read the words in Exercise A on page 25. Help students sound out the words as needed. Remind students that the words in Exercise C must make sense in the sentences.

Optional Activities
• Have students identify and write the names of objects in the room that have the long *a* sound or end with *–ain* or *–ame.*

• Homework: Encourage students to add words that have the long a sound or end with *–ain* or *–ame* to their vocabulary journals.

Back to the Story   Pages 26–28
Follow the outcomes and procedures on page 87 of this guide to teach these pages. Adapt the activities to include asking the following additional question: Why didn't Star and Ray buy a bedroom set from Mr. Silva?

Comprehension: Think and Write   Page 28
Follow the outcomes and procedures on page 87 of this guide to teach these pages.

Comprehension Skills: Comparing and Contrasting   Page 29
• Go over the information and examples in the box with students. Tell students that if they can't find any clue words, they should ask themselves whether the things being compared are alike or different.

Writing Skills: Comparisons   Pages 30–31
• Read the words in the box with students. Explain that the *–er* ending means "more" and the *–est* ending means "most."

Life Skill: Reading a Payment Schedule   Page 32
• Ask students to define the words at the top of the page. Define any words they don't remember. Ask students to find the amount financed, the total amount paid, and the amount of the monthly payment. Help them as needed.

Unit Review   Page 33
Student Outcome: The student will demonstrate mastery of the vocabulary, phonics, and writing skills covered in the unit.

III. WORKBOOK
Assign Workbook Five, Unit 2, pages 11–18.

UNIT 3 • (Pages 34-49)

Sharing Cultures: "Music for the World"

I. STORY OVERVIEW

Today world music is very popular. World music combines traditions from different parts of the world. The Buena Vista Social Club, Värttinä, Papa Wemba, and Angelique Kidjo are famous for playing world music.

II. OUTCOMES AND PROCEDURES

Unit Opener   Pages 34–35

Follow the outcomes and procedures on page 86 of this guide to teach these pages.

Review Words   Page 36

The 12 previously-taught sight words are: *tune, players, different, records, group, fans, countries, listen, meet, people, enjoy, together.*
Follow the outcomes and procedures on page 86 of this guide to teach this page.

Sight Words   Pages 37–39

The 12 new sight words are: *musicians, songs, popular, died, world, style, instruments, live, tradition, combine, melodies, rhythms.*
Follow the outcomes and procedures on page 86 of this guide to teach these pages. Adapt the original activities to include:
• Explain that the names of places are written with a capital letter. Tell students that describing words made from the names of places, such as *Scottish*, are also capitalized.

Phonics   Pages 40–41

Student Outcome: The student will read and write words that end in *–ie* and *–ice* and other words that have the long *i* sound.

Procedures
1. Have students read the words in Exercises A and C on page 40. Help students sound out the words as needed. Remind students that the words in Exercises B and D must make sense in the sentences.

2. Have students read the words in Exercise A on page 41. Help students sound out the words as needed. Remind students that the words in Exercise C must make sense in the sentences.

Optional Activities
• Have students identify and write the names of objects or people in the room whose names end with *–ie* or *–ice* or have the long *i* sound.
• <u>Homework:</u> Encourage students to add words that end with *–ie* or *–ice* or have the long *i* sound to their vocabulary journals.

Back to the Story   Pages 42–44

Follow the outcomes and procedures on page 87 of this guide to teach these pages. Adapt the activities to include asking the following additional question: How does Angelique Kidjo use her African roots in her music?

Comprehension: Think and Write Page 44

Follow the outcomes and procedures on page 87 of this guide to teach these pages.

Comprehension Skills: Sequence Page 45

• Go over the information and examples in the box with students. Tell students that sometimes they can tell the sequence of events by thinking about what event caused another. The cause always comes first, and the event it caused comes afterward.

Writing Skills: Writing a Friendly Letter Pages 46–47

• Have students read the letter and envelope. Have students identify the date, greeting, body, and ending in the letter and the return address and mailing address on the envelope.

Life Skill: Reading a Map   Page 48

• Read the information in the box to the students. Explain to students that on a map north is at the top, south is at the bottom, east is to the right, and west is to the left.

Unit Review   Page 49
Student Outcome: The student will demonstrate mastery of the vocabulary, phonics, and writing skills covered in the unit.

III.   WORKBOOK
Assign Workbook Five, Unit 3, pages 19–26.

UNIT 4 • (Pages 50-65)
Teaching Children About Safety: "A Safe Home"

I.   STORY OVERVIEW
Kim and her two kids live in a neighborhood that is not safe, and Kim is worried. All the parents who live in the building meet together. They ask the building's owners to do some things to help keep their kids safe, and the owners agree.

II.   OUTCOMES AND PROCEDURES
Unit Opener   Pages 50–51
Follow the outcomes and procedures on page 86 of this guide to teach these pages.

Review Words   Page 52
The 12 previously-taught sight words are: *kids, never, could, or, always, every, late, mean, party, club, once, around.*
Follow the outcome, procedures, and optional activities on page 86 of this guide to teach this page.

Sight Words   Pages 53–55
The 12 new sight words are: *show, very, guard, protect, watch, any, strangers, grounds, kind, town, alone, worry.*
Follow the outcomes, procedures, and optional activities on page 86 of this guide to teach these pages. Adapt the original activities to include:
• Review the difference between statements and questions (declarative and interrogative sentences). Ask students to change the declarative sentences in Exercise B on page 53 into interrogative sentences (Is it very safe for kids to play here?).

Phonics   Pages 56–57
Student Outcome: The student will read and write words that end in *–ound* and *–own* and other words with the *ou* and *ow* vowel sounds.

Procedures
1. Have students read the words in Exercises A and C on page 56. Help students sound out the words as needed. Remind students that the words in Exercises B and D must make sense in the sentences.
2. Have students read the words in Exercise A on page 57. Help students to identify the letters that stand for the vowel sounds. Remind students that the words in Exercise E must make sense in the sentences.

Optional Activities
• Have students identify and write the names of objects or people in the room whose names end with *–ound* or *–own* or have the *ou* or *ow* vowel sound.
• Homework: Encourage students to add words that end with *–ound* or *–own* or have the vowel sounds *ou* or *ow* to their vocabulary journals.

Back to the Story   Pages 58–60
Follow the outcomes and procedures on page 87 of this guide to teach these pages. Adapt the activities to include asking the following additional question: Why does Kim think most people in the building will be responsible and try to help?

Comprehension: Think and Write Page 60
Follow the outcomes and procedures on page 87 of this guide to teach these pages.

Comprehension Skills: Inference Page 61
• Go over the information and example in the box with students. Tell students that to test an inference, they should make sure it fits all the facts.

Writing Skills: Adding Endings to *–y* Words   Pages 62–63
• Go over the information in the box with students. Point out that changing the *y* to *i* does

not change the sound of the word because in these words *y* and *i* sound the same.

Life Skill: Telephone Safety   Page 64
• Ask students to define the words at the top of the page. Define any words they don't remember. Read the tips in Exercise A to students or have them read.

Unit Review   Page 65
Student Outcome: The student will demonstrate mastery of the vocabulary, phonics, and writing skills covered in the unit.

III. WORKBOOK
Assign Workbook Five, Unit 4, pages 27–34.

UNIT 5 • (Pages 66-81)
Reaching Your Potential: "Some Really Good 'Failures'"

I.   STORY OVERVIEW
Carla is worried about her son Rocky. He is having trouble in ninth grade because he is a slow reader. Carla orders a video about famous people who were not successful at first. Rocky watches the video and gives a successful report at school about people who have overcome problems.

II.   OUTCOMES AND PROCEDURES
Unit Opener   Pages 66–67
Follow the outcomes and procedures on page 86 of this guide to teach these pages.

Review Words   Page 68
The 12 previously-taught sight words are: *school, ninth, because, wrong, interest, always, slowly, listen, knew, problems, desk, cope.* Follow the outcome, procedures, and optional activities on page 86 of this guide to teach this page.

Sight Words   Pages 69–71
The 13 new sight words are: *joy, failure, those, programs, just, spoil, really, success, brace, impulse, answer, order, famous.*

Follow the outcomes, procedures, and optional activities on page 86 of this guide to teach these pages. Adapt the original activities to include:
• Explain that *mom* is written with a capital *M* if it is used as a name: It was a good impulse, Mom. If a word showing possession *(my, her, his, our, their)* precedes *mom*, it is written with a small *m:* His mom helped him.

Phonics   Pages 72–73
Student Outcome: The student will review and identify words that end in –*oil* and –*oy* and other words with the *oi* and *oy* vowel sound.

Procedures
1. Have students read the words in Exercises A and C on page 72. Help students sound out the words as needed. Remind students that the words in Exercises B and D must make sense in the sentence.
2. Have students read the words in Exercises A and B on page 73. Point out to students that *oi* and *oy* stand for the same vowel sound. Remind students that the words in Exercise C must make sense in the sentence.

Optional Activities
• Have students identify and write the names of objects or people in the room whose names end with –*oil* or –*oy* or have the *oi* or *oy* vowel sounds.
• Homework: Encourage students to add words that end with –*oil* or –*oy* or have the *oi* or *oy* vowel sound to their vocabulary journals.

Back to the Story   Pages 74–76
Follow the outcomes and procedures on page 87 of this guide to teach these pages. Adapt the activities to include asking the following additional question: Why was Carla careful not to say anything more to Rocky about working for success?

Comprehension: Think and Write Page 76
Follow the outcomes and procedures on page 87 of this guide to teach these pages.

Comprehension Skills: Making Judgements   Page 77

• Go over the information in the box with students. Tell students that the judgments they make about the reading are personal, and that their judgments may be different from their classmates'.

Writing Skills: Plural Possessive Nouns   Pages 78–79

• Go over the information and examples in the box with students. Point out that the apostrophe added for the plural possessive does not change the way the word sounds.

Life Skill: Reading a Chart   Page 80

• Ask students to define the words in Exercise A. Define any words they don't remember. Ask students to identify the categories of information in the table: name, problem, and success.

Unit Review   Page 81

Student Outcome: The student will demonstrate mastery of the vocabulary, phonics, and writing skills covered in the unit.

III.   WORKBOOK

Assign Workbook Five, Unit 5, pages 35–42.

UNIT 6 • (Pages 82-97)

Following Immigration Procedures: "A Home Away From Home"

I.   STORY OVERVIEW

The main character, an immigrant, is happy in the U.S., but she misses her sister Rose. Rose comes for a visit. Then she gets a job in the U.S., too.

II.   OUTCOMES AND PROCEDURES

Unit Opener   Pages 82–83

Follow the outcomes and procedures on page 86 of this guide to teach these pages.

Review Words   Page 84

The 12 previously-taught sight words are: *picked, here, sweeping, if, been, before, cooking,*

then, sentence, year, blues, thinking.
Follow the outcome, procedures, and optional activities on page 86 of this guide to teach this page.

Sight Words   Pages 85–87

The 12 new sight words are: *visit, permission, immigration, green, American, employer, goes, house, call, legal, draw, papers.*
Follow the outcomes, procedures, and optional activities on page 86 of this guide to teach these pages. Adapt the original activities to include:
• Remind students that in contractions, the apostrophe stands for the missing letters. For example, in *doesn't,* the apostrophe stands for *o.* Ask students to look for other examples and write them as separate, complete words.

Phonics   Pages 88–89

Student Outcome: Students will review and identify words that end in *–all* and *–aw.* Students will divide words into syllables and identify syllables with the schwa vowel sound.

Procedures

1. Have students read the words in Exercises A and C on page 88. Help students sound out the words as needed. Remind students that the words in Exercises B and D must make sense in the sentences.
2. Have students sound out the words in Exercise A on page 89. Tell students that schwa sounds like *uh.* Remind students that the words in Exercise E must make sense in the sentences.

Optional Activities

• Have students identify and write the names of objects or people in the room whose names end with *–all* or *–aw.* Encourage students to add the words to their vocabulary journals.
• Homework: Encourage students to look back at the words in their vocabulary journals and divide them into syllables.

Back to the Story   Pages 90–92

Follow the outcomes and procedures on page 87 of this guide to teach these pages. Adapt the activities to include asking the following additional question: Why does Rose need to get her green card?

Comprehension: Think and Write   Page 92

Follow the outcomes and procedures on page 87 of this guide to teach these pages.

Comprehension Skills: Drawing Conclusions   Page 93

• Go over the information in the box with students. Point out to students that all the facts must support the conclusion.

Writing Skills: Irregular Verbs   Pages 94–95

• Go over the information and examples in the box with students. Explain that irregular verbs must be memorized.

Life Skill: Filling Out a Form   Page 96

• Ask students to define the words in Exercise A. Define any words they don't remember. Go over the form with students.

Unit Review   Page 97

Student Outcome: The student will demonstrate mastery of the vocabulary, phonics, and writing skills covered in the unit.

III.   WORKBOOK

Assign Workbook Five, Unit 6, pages 43–50.

UNIT 7 • (Pages 98-113)

Handling Social Relationships: "Will They Meet?"

I.   STORY OVERVIEW

Pedro wants to meet Ana, a woman who works in a card shop, but he doesn't know how. He keeps going back to buy more cards he doesn't need. Finally Pedro gives a card to Ana, and they become friends.

II.   OUTCOMES AND PROCEDURES

Unit Opener   Pages 98–99

Follow the outcomes and procedures on page 86 of this guide to teach these pages.

Review Words   Page 100

The 12 previously-taught sight words are: *saw, must, summer, how, soon, thank, too, ask, would, why, card, better.*
Follow the outcome, procedures, and optional activities on page 86 of this guide to teach this page.

Sight Words   Pages 101–103

The 12 new sight words are: *noticed, girl, start, true, idea, few, birthday, open, wish, please, far, warm.*
Follow the outcomes and procedures on page 86 of this guide to teach these pages. Adapt the original activities to include:
• Discuss expressions whose meaning cannot be derived from its words (idioms), such as *gave him a start.* Ask the students to explain the idiom. Have them look for other examples. Have the students write the examples in their journals.

Phonics   Pages 104–105

Student Outcome: The student will review and identify words that end in *–ue* and *–ew* and words with the *–oo* and *–oo* vowel sounds.

Procedures
1. Have students read the words in Exercises A and C on page 104. Help students sound out the words as needed. Remind students that the words in Exercises B and D must make sense in the sentences.
2. Have students read the words in Exercises A and C on page 105. Point out to students that although the vowel sounds are spelled differently, they are pronounced the same. Remind students that the words in Exercise E must make sense in the sentences.

Optional Activities
- Have students identify and write the names of objects or people in the room whose names end with *–ue* or *–ew* or have the vowel sounds *–oo* or *–oo*.
- <u>Homework:</u> Encourage students to add words that end with *–ue* or *–ew* or have the vowel sounds *–oo* or *–oo* to their vocabulary journals.

Back to the Story   Pages 106–108
Follow the outcomes and procedures on page 87 of this guide to teach these pages. Adapt the activities to include asking the following additional question: Why was Pedro glad Ana was alone when he gave her the card?

Comprehension: Think and Write Page 108
Follow the outcomes and procedures on page 87 of this guide to teach these pages.

Comprehension Skills: Classifying Page 109
- Go over the information in the box with students. Tell students that classifying makes information easier to understand.

Writing Skills: Reflexive Pronouns Pages 110–111
- Go over the examples in the box with students. Help students pronounce *self* and *selves.*

Life Skill: Reading a Menu   Page 112
- Ask students to define the words at the top of the page. Define any words they don't remember. Ask students to identify the categories in the menu: *sandwiches, diet delight, grill, dinner salad, beverages, desserts, and extras.*

Unit Review   Page 113
Student Outcome: The student will demonstrate mastery of the vocabulary, phonics, and writing skills covered in the unit.

III. WORKBOOK
Assign Workbook Five, Unit 7, pages 51–58.

CONCLUDING THE BOOK

Final Review   Pages 114–117
Student Outcome: The student will demonstrate mastery of the vocabulary, phonics, and writing skills covered in Book 5.

At Your Leisure   Pages 118–119
Student Outcome: The student will read the poem and the related prose passage for enjoyment.

Procedures
1. Have students read the poem and story, or read it with them. Help them with any unfamiliar words. Encourage them to talk about what they have read.
2. Talk about the What Do You Think question together or have students write their answer.

Book Six

Overview

Book Six, written at the 5.0–6.0 reading level, continues the seven-unit structure of the *Reading for Today* program. In addition, Book Six introduces two new types of lesson pages, Vocabulary and Word Study. The lesson plan for Unit 1 is complete, and it is the model for the units that follow. For Units 2–7, refer to Unit 1 where indicated in the lesson plans for those units.

UNIT 1 • (Pages 2-19)

Communicating Ideas: "One Woman, Two Worlds"

I.   STORY OVERVIEW

The profile of Latina writer Sandra Cisneros tells how she grew up in two different worlds, the world of U.S. culture and the world of Latino culture. Cisneros writes stories about both these worlds. Her stories help people from the two worlds to understand each other.

II.   OUTCOMES AND PROCEDURES

Unit Opener   Pages 2–3

Student Outcome: The student will apply prior knowledge and predicting skills to a new reading selection.

Procedures

1. Read the unit title and the Discussion box with students. Discuss the story title and the photo.
2. Have students read the beginning of the story and predict what will happen in the rest of the story.

Vocabulary: Definitions   Page 5

Student Outcome: The student will demonstrate recognition of 10 new vocabulary words: *audience, childhood, commitment, culture, passion, conflict, influences, poem, relatives, tradition.*

Procedures

1. Read each vocabulary word aloud and have students repeat it.
2. Have students complete the activities. Then check the answers together.
3. Remind students that context clues can help them to determine the definitions of new words. Tell them to look for words before or after the new word that express the same idea.

Vocabulary: Multiple Meanings   Page 6

Student Outcome: The student will choose the appropriate meaning of the words *border* and *hard* for the context.

Procedures

1. Go over the instructions and the meanings for border and hard with students.
2. Help students as needed with Exercises A and B and check the answers together.
3. Point out to students that some words, such as *border,* can be either nouns or verbs.

Word Study: Dividing Words into Syllables   Page 7

Student Outcome: The student will divide words with the VCCV (vowel-consonant-consonant-vowel) pattern into syllables.

Procedures

1. Go over the information and examples in the box with students.
2. Go over the instructions with students and help them as needed with the activity.

Optional Activities

• Have students identify and write the names of objects in the room that have the VCCV pattern.
• Homework: Encourage students to add words with the VCCV pattern to their vocabulary journals.

Back to the Story   Pages 8–12

Student Outcomes: The student will apply recalling and predicting skills and read new sight words in context.

Procedures

1. Read the question on page 8 with the students. Ask students to review what they have learned in the story thus far. Have students look at the picture and predict what they think the rest of the story will be about.
2. Have students read the story on pages 8–12. Help with any words the students do not recognize.
3. Ask the students the following question: Why do you think coming of age in the U.S. might be hard for children of other cultures?

Comprehension: Think and Write
Page 12

Student Outcomes: The student will apply basic comprehension skills (main idea, details, sequence, inference, cause and effect, and drawing conclusions) to understanding the story; summarize the information in the story, and relate ideas to the student's own experience.

Procedures

1. Read the questions in Think About It to the students or have them read. Help students answer questions. Review the story if necessary to help students find information to support answers.
2. Ask students to express their opinion when they answer the question in Write About It. Assign pages 132–139, The Writing Process. After students complete this section, have them use the steps in the writing process when they respond to the Write About It topic. Help students with their writing as necessary.

Comprehension Skills: Recalling Facts
Page 13

Student Outcomes: Students will recall facts from the story.

Procedures

1. Read the instructions with students. Remind students to be careful to fill in the correct circle for their answer choice.
2. Review the answers with students.

Comprehension Skills: Character Traits
Pages 14–15

Student Outcomes: Students will correctly identify character traits.

Procedures

• Read the information and tips at the top of page 14 with students. Go over the exercise instructions with students and discuss their answers.

Writing Skills: Using Adjectives
Pages 16–17

• Go over the information in the box with students. Explain that adjectives always tell about nouns.

Life Skill: Finding Library Materials
Page 18

• Read the information in the box with learners. Help them with any words they don't understand.
• Go over the exercise instructions with students and check their answers.

Unit Review   Page 19

Student Outcome: The student will demonstrate mastery of the vocabulary, phonics, and writing skills covered in the unit.

III. WORKBOOK

Assign Workbook Six, Unit 1, pages 3–12.

UNIT 2 • (Pages 20-37)

Using Technology: "Moving Ahead"

I. STORY OVERVIEW

Ralph works at the check-out counter of a grocery store. He likes the store, but he doesn't make enough money for his family. Ralph talks to his boss, and the boss sends Ralph to computer classes so he can take a better job in the store.

II. OUTCOMES AND PROCEDURES
Unit Opener   Pages 20–22

Follow the outcomes and procedures on page 95 of this guide to teach these pages.

Vocabulary: Definitions in Context
Page 23

Student Outcome: The student will demonstrate recognition of 10 new vocabulary words: *productive, reliable, ambition, requirements, accuracy, circulars, convenient, frequently, inventory, access.*

Follow the outcomes, procedures, and optional activities on page 95 of this guide to teach this page.

Vocabulary: Word Stress   Page 24

Student Outcomes: The student will choose the correct meaning and word stress for the context.

Procedures

1. Go over the instructions and the words in Exercise A with students.
2. Have students complete Exercise B and check the answers together.
3. Point out to students that some words are pronounced differently depending on whether they are being used as nouns or verbs.

Word Study: Dividing Words into Syllables—the VCV pattern   Page 25

Student Outcome: The student will divide words with the VCV (vowel-consonant-vowel) pattern into syllables.

Procedures

1. Go over the information and examples in the box with students.
2. Go over the instructions with students and help them as needed with the activities.

Optional Activities

• Have students identify and write the names of objects in the room that have the VCV pattern.
• Homework: Encourage students to add words with the VCV pattern to their vocabulary journals.

Back to the Story   Pages 26–30

Follow the outcomes and procedures on pages 95–96 of this guide to teach these pages. Adapt the activities to include asking the following additional question: After Ralph completed

the computer course, why didn't he look for a job at a bigger store where he could make more money?

Comprehension: Think and Write
Page 30

Follow the outcomes and procedures on page 96 of this guide to teach these pages.

Comprehension Skills: Recalling Facts/Main Idea   Page 31

Student Outcomes: Students will recall facts from the story and identify the main idea.

Use the procedures on page 96 of this guide to teach this page.

Comprehension Skills: Cause and Effect
Pages 32–33

Student Outcomes: Students will correctly identify causes and effects.

Procedures

• Read the information in the box with students. Go over the exercise instructions and check students' answers.

Writing Skills: Writing Names and Titles
Pages 34–35

• Go over the information in the box with students. Explain that capitalization rules must be memorized.

Life Skill: Reading Abbreviations
Page 36

• Read the information at the top of the page with learners. Help them with any words they don't understand.
• Go over the exercise instructions with students and check their answers.

Unit Review   Page 37

Student Outcome: The student will demonstrate mastery of the vocabulary, phonics, and writing skills covered in the unit.

III. WORKBOOK

Assign Workbook Six, Unit 2, pages 13–22.

UNIT 3 • (Pages 38-55)

Understanding Self and Others: "Body Language"

I. STORY OVERVIEW

Body language is an important way of communicating. Being aware of your own body language can help you send the right message. Being aware of others' body language can help you to understand them better.

II. OUTCOMES AND PROCEDURES

Unit Opener Pages 38–40

Follow the outcomes and procedures on page 95 of this guide to teach these pages.

Vocabulary: Definitions Page 41

Student Outcome: The student will demonstrate recognition of 10 new vocabulary words: *behavior, facial, gesture, nonverbal, posture, communication, conscious, insight, observe, reveal.*

Follow the outcomes, procedures, and optional activities on page 95 of this guide to teach this page.

Vocabulary: Prefixes and Suffixes Page 42

Student Outcome: The student will read and write words with the prefix *–un* and the suffix *–ness.*

Procedures
1. Go over the information in the box and the word lists with students.
2. Help students as needed with Exercises A and B and check the answers together.
3. Explain to students that words with the prefix *un–* are usually adjectives, and that words with the suffix *–ness* are nouns.

Word Study: Dividing Words into Syllables-Consonant + *le* Pattern Page 43

Student Outcome: The student will divide words with the consonant + *le* pattern into syllables.

Procedures
1. Go over the information and examples in the box with students.
2. Go over the instructions with students and help them as needed with the activities.

Optional Activities
• Have students identify and write the names of objects in the room that have the consonant + *le* pattern.
• Homework: Encourage students to add words with the consonant + *le* pattern to their vocabulary journals.

Back to the Story Pages 44–48

Follow the outcomes and procedures on pages 95–96 of this guide to teach these pages. Adapt the activities to include asking the following additional question: Why is it important not to use take-charge body language that is too strong?

Comprehension: Think and Write Page 48

Follow the outcomes and procedures on page 96 of this guide to teach these pages.

Comprehension Skills: Recalling Facts Page 49

Use the outcomes and procedures on page 96 of this guide to teach this page.

Comprehension Skills: Inference Pages 50–51

Student Outcomes: Students will make correct inferences.

Procedures
• Read the information in the box with students. Go over the exercise instructions with students and check their answers.

Writing Skills: Writing Complete Sentences Pages 52–53

• Go over the information in the box with students. Explain that a sentence must have a subject and a predicate to be complete.

Life Skill: Writing a Summary of Qualifications Page 54
• Read the information in the box with learners. Help them with any words they don't understand.
• Go over the exercise instructions with students and check their answers.

Unit Review Page 55
Student Outcome: The student will demonstrate mastery of the vocabulary, word study, and writing skills covered in the unit.

III. WORKBOOK
Assign Workbook Six, Unit 3, pages 23–32.

UNIT 4 • (Pages 56-73)
Reaching Your Potential: "Amazing Mary"

I. STORY OVERVIEW
Dr. Mary Groda-Lewis came from a poor family. She didn't do well in school because she had trouble learning to read and write. As a teenager, she got in trouble with the law. Still, she overcame these and other obstacles to become a doctor.

II. OUTCOMES AND PROCEDURES
Unit Opener Pages 56–58
Follow the outcomes and procedures on page 95 of this guide to teach these pages.

Vocabulary: Definitions Page 59
Student Outcome: The student will demonstrate recognition of 10 new vocabulary words: *conceal, dedication, physician, sensitive, severe, assist, disability, overcome, resent, unbearable.*

Follow the outcomes and procedures on page 95 of this guide to teach this page.

Vocabulary: Antonyms Page 60
Student Outcome: The student will recognize and identify antonyms.

Procedures
1. Go over the information in the box with students.
2. Help students as needed with Exercises A and B and check the answers together.
3. Remind students to use context clues to make sure of the meanings of the words in Exercise B.

Word Study: Dictionary Entries Page 61
Student Outcome: The student will read and understand a dictionary entry.

Procedures
1. Go over the information and example in the box with students.
2. Go over the instructions with students and help them as needed with the activities.

Optional Activities
• Have students choose other words from the dictionary, read the entries, and write sentences with the words.
• Homework: Encourage students to add the words they looked up in the dictionary to their vocabulary journals.

Back to the Story Pages 62–66
Follow the outcomes and procedures on pages 95–96 of this guide to teach these pages. Adapt the activities to include asking the following additional question: Why did the nurses in the hospital in Youngstown like Mary?

Comprehension: Think and Write Page 66
Follow the outcomes and procedures on page 96 of this guide to teach these pages.

Comprehension Skills: Recalling Facts/Main Idea Page 67
Student Outcomes: Students will recall facts from the story and identify the main idea.

Use the procedures on page 96 of this guide to teach this page.

Comprehension Skills: Sequence
Pages 68–69

Student Outcomes: Students will identify the sequence of events from the story.

Procedures

• Read the information in the box with students. Go over the exercise instructions with students and check their answers.

Writing Skills: Recognizing Fragments
Pages 70–71

• Go over the information in the box with students. Point out to students that to tell whether to add a subject or a predicate to a fragment, ask whether the fragment describes a thing, person, or idea (subject) or an action (predicate).

Life Skill: Completing a Medical Form
Page 72

• Read the information in the box with learners. Help them with any words they don't understand.
• Go over the exercise instructions with students and check their answers.

Unit Review   Page 73

Student Outcome: The student will demonstrate mastery of the vocabulary, word study, and writing skills covered in the unit.

III. WORKBOOK

Assign Workbook Six, Unit 4, pages 33–42.

UNIT 5 • *(Pages 74-91)*
Using Credit: "Charge It!"

I.   STORY OVERVIEW

The story uses Fred and Anita's purchase on credit of a washing machine as an example to discuss credit checks, interest, and cleaning up bad credit.

II.   OUTCOMES AND PROCEDURES
Unit Opener   Pages 74–76

Follow the outcomes and procedures on page 95 of this guide to teach these pages.

Vocabulary: Definitions Page 77

Student Outcome: The student will demonstrate recognition of 10 new vocabulary words: *accurate, apply, establish, financial, installment, notify, obligation, previous, qualify, reference.*

Follow the outcomes, procedures, and optional activities on page 95 of this guide to teach this page.

Vocabulary: Suffixes   Page 78

Student Outcome: The student will demonstrate recognition of the suffixes *–er* and *–or.*

Procedures

1. Go over the information in the box with students.
2. Help students as needed with the exercise and check the answers together.
3. Tell students that they must memorize which words add *–er* and which add *–or.*

Word Study: Prefixes and Suffixes
Page 79

Student Outcome: The student will divide words with prefixes and suffixes into syllables.

Procedures

1. Go over the information and examples in the box with students.
2. Go over the instructions with students and help them as needed with the activities.

Optional Activities

• Have students think of other words with more than one prefix or suffix and divide them into syllables.
• Homework: Encourage students to add the words with more than one prefix or suffix to their vocabulary journals.

Back to the Story   Pages 80–84

Follow the outcomes and procedures on pages 95–96 of this guide to teach these pages. Adapt the activities to include asking the following additional question: What can you do if you have a bad credit record?

Comprehension: Think and Write   Page 84

Follow the outcomes and procedures on page 96 of this guide to teach these pages.

Comprehension Skills: Recalling Facts/Cause and Effect   Page 85

Student Outcomes: Students will recall facts from the story and identify causes and effects.

Use the procedures on page 96 of this guide to teach this page.

Comprehension Skills: Drawing Conclusions   Pages 86–87

Student Outcomes: Students will draw accurate conclusions.

Procedures
• Read the information in the box with students. Go over the exercise instructions with students and check their answers.

Writing Skills: Past Tense of Verbs   Pages 88–89

• Go over the information in the box with students. Explain to students that the helping verb in the past participle form must agree with its subject (I have, she has).

Life Skill: Filling Out a Credit Application   Page 90

• Read the information in the box with learners. Help them with any words they don't understand.
• Go over the exercise instructions with students and check their answers.

Unit Review   Page 91

Student Outcome: The student will demonstrate mastery of the vocabulary, word study, and writing skills covered in the unit.

III.   WORKBOOK

Assign Workbook Six, Unit 5, pages 43–52.

UNIT 6 • (Pages 92-109)

Working with Others: "A Problem in the Workplace"

I.   STORY OVERVIEW

It can be difficult to tell what situations constitute sexual harassment. The two types of sexual harassment recognized by courts are *quid pro quo* and those that result in a hostile work environment. Workers suffering sexual harassment can make a complaint to their employer or go to court.

II.   OUTCOMES AND PROCEDURES

Unit Opener   Pages 92–94

Follow the outcomes and procedures on page 95 of this guide to teach these pages.

Vocabulary: Definitions   Page 95

Student Outcome: The student will demonstrate recognition of 10 new vocabulary words: *conditions, emotions, environment, hostile, offensive, constitute, harassment, promotion, representative, supervisor.*

Follow the outcomes, procedures, and optional activities on page 95 of this guide to teach this page.

Vocabulary: Analogies   Page 96

Student Outcome: The student will complete analogies.

Procedures
1. Go over the information in the box with students.
2. Help students as needed with the exercise and check the answers together.
3. Tell students the analogies may be easier to complete if they classify them by types.

Word Study: Pronunciation   Page 97

Student Outcome: The student will use a pronunciation key to pronounce words.

Procedures

1. Go over the information in the box with students.
2. Go over the instructions with students and help them as needed with the activities.

Optional Activities

• Have students choose a few unfamiliar words from the dictionary and copy down their phonetic spellings.

• Homework: Encourage students to add the words and their phonetic spellings to their vocabulary journals.

Back to the Story   Pages 98–102

Follow the outcomes and procedures on pages 95–96 of this guide to teach these pages. Adapt the activities to include asking the following additional question: How do training sessions help companies avoid the problem of sexual harassment?

Comprehension: Think and Write Page 102

Follow the outcomes and procedures on page 96 of this guide to teach these pages.

Comprehension Skills: Recalling Facts/Character Traits   Page 103

Student Outcomes: Students will recall facts from the story and identify character traits.
Use the procedures on page 96 of this guide to teach this page.

Comprehension Skills: Writer's Tone and Purpose   Pages 104–105

Student Outcomes: Students will recognize a writer's tone and purpose.

Procedures

• Read the information in the box with students. Go over the exercise instructions with students and check their answers.

Writing Skills: Pronouns Pages 106–107

• Go over the information in the box with students. Remind students that *they* and *them* are plural pronouns, and can only take the place of plural subjects and objects.

Life Skill: Being a Good Listener Page 108

• Read the information in the box with learners. Help them with any words they don't understand.
• Go over the exercise instructions with students and check their answers.

Unit Review   Page 109

Student Outcome: The student will demonstrate mastery of the vocabulary, word study, and writing skills covered in the unit.

III.   WORKBOOK

Assign Workbook Six, Unit 6, pages 53–63.

UNIT 7 • (Pages 110-127)

Reaching Your Potential: "Oprah's Journey"

I.   STORY OVERVIEW

Oprah Winfrey was born on a Mississippi farm to an unwed teenage mother. She has overcome many obstacles to become an American legend. People love her show because they know she understands them.

II.   OUTCOMES AND PROCEDURES

Unit Opener   Pages 110–112

Follow the outcomes and procedures on page 95 of this guide to teach these pages.

Vocabulary: Definitions   Page 113

Student Outcome: The student will demonstrate recognition of 10 new vocabulary words: *achievements, poverty, literacy, spirituality, legend, executive, discipline, charity, challenge, empathy.*

Follow the outcomes, procedures, and optional activities on page 95 of this guide to teach this page.

Vocabulary: Prefixes   Page 114
Student Outcome: The student will read and write words with common prefixes.

Procedures
1. Go over the information in the box with students.
2. Help students as needed with the exercise and check the answers together.
3. Explain to students that *in–* and *im–* are really the same prefix, but the *n* changes to an *m* in front of some letters.

Word Study: Accent Marks   Page 115
Student Outcome: The student will read and write accent marks in words to show which syllable is stressed.

Procedures
1. Go over the information in the box with students.
2. Go over the instructions with students and help them as needed with the activities.

Optional Activities
• Have students think of other words that change their stress when they change meaning. Ask students to write sentences for both meanings.
• Homework: Encourage students to add the words that change their stress when they change meaning to their vocabulary journals.

Back to the Story   Pages 116–120
Follow the outcomes and procedures on pages 95–96 of this guide to teach these pages. Adapt the activities to include asking the following additional question: Why did Oprah start her book club?

Comprehension: Think and Write Page 120
Follow the outcomes and procedures on page 96 of this guide to teach these pages.

Comprehension Skills: Recalling Facts/Writer's Tone and Purpose   Page 121
Student Outcomes: Students will recall facts from the story and identify the writer's tone and purpose.

Use the procedures on page 96 of this guide to teach this page.

Comprehension Skills: Fact vs. Opinion Pages 122–123
Student Outcomes: Students will distinguish between facts and opinions.

Procedures
• Read the information in the box with students. Go over the exercise instructions with students and check their answers.

Writing Skills: Recognizing Run-ons Pages 124–125
• Go over the information in the box with students. Point out to students that run-ons have two subjects and two predicates.

Life Skill: Using an Index   Page 126
• Read the information in the box with learners. Help them with any words they don't understand.
• Go over the exercise instructions with students and check their answers.

Unit Review   Page 127
Student Outcome: The student will demonstrate mastery of the vocabulary, word study, and writing skills covered in the unit.

III. WORKBOOK
Assign Unit 7, pages 64–73.

CONCLUDING THE BOOK

Final Review   Pages 128–131
Student Outcome: The student will demonstrate mastery of the vocabulary, word study, and writing skills covered in Book Six.

The Writing Process   Pages 132–139

Student Outcome: The student will be able to use the steps in the writing process to complete the Write About It activity in each unit.

• Assign this section before the student completes Write About It for Unit 1, page 12.

• Discuss each of the steps in the process with students and then have them complete the activity for that step.

• For each Write About It in Units 2–7, refer students to this section. Have them review the steps in the writing process, then use the steps as they write.

Unit 1

Page 3

2.
A	O	A	C	A	F
R	A	P	F	A	
a	o	c	g	c	a
e	a	p	c	a	a
at	can	ran	Ann	Al	and	an

3.
B	A	B	P	B	D
R	B	A	R	B	
b	g	b	a	b	p
o	b	c	p	g	b
bat	cab	Bob	big	Bess	web

Page 4

2.
C	O	G	C	C
D	B	G	C	O
c	o	c	a	c	e
o	c	a	e	c	
cat	cab	bacon	Cass	Cal

3.
D	B	C	D	G
P	B	D	D	P
d	a	d	d	c
b	p	b	d	p	b
dog	bad	Dad	red	and	Dot

Page 5

2.
E	A	E	P	E
F	T	E	F	T
c	e	o	e	e
c	a	e	o	c	e
Ella	bed	get	egg	Ed	red

3.
F	B	F	P	F
F	E	T	F	E
f	h	f	b	f	t
f	f	t	b	h	f
fan	Fran	if	fun	Jeff	Fred

Page 6

3.
A	B	C	D	E	F
a	b	c	d	e	f

4.
A	b	D	f	B	c
E	d	C	a	F	e

5.
Bob	bat	box	lab	cab
cut	cap	cat	cub	back

Page 7

2.
G	C	G	C	D
G	O	C	G	.
g	q	g	c	g
p	q	g	j	p	g
Gus	egg	got	Peg	dog	gas

3.
H	E	H	E	T
H	F	H	T	H
h	b	h	d	p
h	d	h	f	h	d
Hal	hill	had	fish	he	Helen

Page 8

2.
I	E	I	T	I	L
T	I	L	I	E	I
i	i	i	j	h	i
l	j	i	l	l	
i	j	i	l	i	
in	Inez	quit	if	did	is	kite

3.
J	I	J	J	F	T
G	P	J	C	J	J
j	i	j	j	j	g
i	t	f	g	p	i
j	f				
Jan	jog	jam	job	jet	Jim

Page 9

2.
K	T	I	K	K	R
E	F	R	B	K	
k	l	k	k	l	t	f

b	k	d	b	k	f
Ken	kid	kit	sick	Kim	kick

3.

L	L	T	K	L	L
E	T	E	L	F	L
l	h	l	h	l	
t	f	t	k	f	
t	l	h	t	l	
leg	hill	Bill	log	Lin	Allen

Page 10

3.

G	H	I	J	K	L
g	h	i	j	k	l

4.

G	i	J	k	H	h
K	l	I	g	L	j

5.

egg	get	gas	Gus	pig
kick	kit	Kim	Ken	sick

Page 11

2.

M	N	M	W	M	
V	W	M	N		
u	n	u	m	m	n
n	u	m	n	w	w
man	met	Mom	ham	Tom	miss

3.

N	N	M	N	N	
V	M	N	V	M	
n	u	n	u	n	m
v	n	n	m	v	n	u
not	Ned	nut	Nan	net	fun

Page 12

2.

O	Q	O	O	C	
D	Q	O	C		
o	c	o	o	o	
a	c	o	a	c	o
off	on	Mom	not	log	pot

3.

P	B	P	B	P	
P	F	B	R	P	
p	q	p	d	p	
b	q	p	p	b	d
pan	Pam	cup	pop	Pat	pen

Page 13

2.

Q	O	Q	Q	C	
C	O	Q	O		
g	q	q	p	q	
p	q	q	g	p	g
quiet	quit	quiz	Quinn	quilt	

3.

R	P	R	D	R	
P	F	R	B	R	
r	r	n	r	u	f
r	r	n	f	p	r
Rob	ran	red	rug	car	Ron

Page 14

3.

M	N	O	P	Q	R
m	n	o	p	q	r

4.

M	m	P	q	N	o
Q	p	O	n	R	r

5.

man	ham	met	Matt	am
quit	liquid	quick	Quinn	

Page 15

2.

S	G	S	O	S	
B	S	S	J	B	
s	c	s	s	o	e
a	s	c	a	s	e	o
sun	sit	sat	Sam	gas	Sara

3.

T	J	T	I	T	L
F	T	E	I	T	L
t	t	l	i	t	f	l
t	t	i	f	l	t	i
top	tan	Tom	Tess	cat	letter

Page 16

2.

U	C	U	O	U
U	V	N	U	
u	n	u	u	m
v	e	v	u	n	u
us	gum	bus	up	rub	cup

3.

V	W	W	V	N
V	W	M	V	N
y	y	w	y	y
u	w	u	y	w	u
Van	yet	yest	never	Val	very

Page 17

2.

W	M	W	N	W
V	V	W	N	
w	u	v	w	w
v	u	w	v	w	v
wig	Will	wet	win	wax	Walt

3.

X	A	X	V	X
K	K	X	A	K
x	w	x	x	v
k	w	x	x	k	v
ax	six	Rex	tax	wax	box

Page 18

2.

Y	Y	K	Y	I
Y	K	T	K	Y	I
y	w	y	y	p
g	j	y	q	v	y
yes	yet	yell	day	you	very

3.

Z	N	Z	Z	M
Z	E	F	N	Z
z	x	z	z	w
e	v	z	v	w	z
jazz	zip	Liz	buzz	quiz	zigzag

Page 19

3.

S	T	U	V
W	X	Y	Z
s	t	u	v
w	x	y	z

4.

S	v	W	x
T	u	X	w
U	t	Y	z
V	s	Z	y

5.

sis	miss	test	yes	set
yes	yell	yam	yet	very

Page 20

1.

A	B	C	D	E	F	
G	H	I	J	K	L	
M	N	O	P	Q	R	S
T	U	V	W	X	Y	Z

2.

B	h	K	r	W	z
F	b	M	q	S	u
C	a	J	k	X	t
H	i	O	m	T	s
D	f	R	l	Z	w
A	g	L	p	V	x
E	c	Q	o	Y	v
I	d	N	n	U	y
G	e	P	j		

Page 21

1.

a	b	c	d	e	
f	g	h	i	j	
k	l	m	n	o	
p	q	r	s	t	
u	v	w	x	y	z

2.

get	dog	Gus	egg	jog
Rod	rock	dirt	rag	run
dog	bad	nod	Dot	red
Max	miss	ham	Pam	met
Pam	cap	pad	pen	pop

fit   Cl<u>iff</u>   <u>F</u>ran   fa<u>x</u>   <u>f</u>an
Bo<u>b</u>   <u>b</u>ell   we<u>b</u>   <u>B</u>ess   ta<u>b</u>
<u>qu</u>it   <u>qu</u>ick   <u>qu</u>iz   <u>Qu</u>inn <u>qu</u>iet

Page 25

Answers will vary (personal information).

Unit 2

Page 26

B. 1. m *(man)*   2. m *(mat)*
    3. m *(mop)*   4. *(bed)*
    5. *(table)*   6. m *(milk)*
    7. m *(map)*   8. m *(mail)*

C. Answers will vary.

D. 1 man, 2 mat, 3 mop, 6 milk, 7 map, 8 mail

Page 27

B. 1. d *(darts)*   2. *(van)*
    3. d *(desk)*   4. *(mop)*
    5. d *(dam)*   6. d *(dishes)*
    7. d *(door)*   8. d *(dice)*

C. Answers will vary.

D. darts, desk, dam, dishes, door, dice

Page 28

B. 1. f *(fish)*   2. *(mail)*
    3. f *(feather)*   4. f *(football)*
    5. f *(fan)*   6. *(apple)*
    7. f *(fork)*   8. f *(fuse)*

C. Answers will vary.

D. fish, feather, football, fan, fork, fuse

Page 29

B. 1. g *(gum)*   2. *(zipper)*
    3. g *(gate)*   4. g *(game)*
    5. g *(gas)*   6. g *(goat)*
    7. g *(guitar)*   8. *(desk)*

C. Answers will vary.

D. gum, gate, game, gas, goat, guitar

Page 30

A. 1. m *(jam)*   2. d *(bread)*
    3. m *(dam)*   4. f *(safe)*
    5. g *(dog)*   6. f *(knife)*
    7. d *(bed)*   8. g *(flag)*

B. 1. m   2. g   3. d   4. f
    5. dam   6. leaf   7. dog   8. mad

Page 31

B. 1. a *(animals)*   2. a *(ant)*
    3. a *(ax)*   4. *(key)*
    5. *(dishes)*   6. a *(astronaut)*
    7. a *(alligator)*   8. a *(apple)*

C. Answers will vary.

D. animals, ant, ax, astronaut, alligator, apple

Page 32

B. 1. a *(gas)*   2. a *(fan)*
    3. a *(can)*   4. *(olive)*
    5. a *(ham)*   6. a *(cat)*
    7. *(egg)*   8. a *(van)*

C. Answers will vary.

D. gas, fan, can, ham, cat, van

Page 33

A. 1. m *(man)*   2. f *(football)*
    3. d *(darts)*   4. g *(go)*
    5. f *(feather)*   6. a *(ax)*
    7. g *(game)*   8. m *(money)*

B. 1. map   2. fan   3. cat

Page 34

1. <u>m</u>op   2. lea<u>f</u>   3. ham   4. da<u>m</u>
5. <u>f</u>an   6. be<u>d</u>   7. <u>m</u>at   8. <u>a</u>x
9. dog   10. m<u>a</u>p   11. gas   12. <u>d</u>esk

Page 35

B. dog, money, food, go, ham, bed, leaf, log, apple, man

C. and D. Answers will vary.

Page 36

B. 1. b *(belt)*   2. b *(bat)*
    3. *(map)*   4. b *(banana)*
    5. *(door)*   6. b *(bus)*
    7. b *(book)*   8. b *(button)*

C. Answers will vary.

D. belt, bat, banana, bus, book, button

Page 37

B. 1. t *(tomato)*   2. t *(tire)*
    3. *(fork)*   4. t *(tie)*
    5. t *(tools)*   6. t *(television)*
    7. t *(toaster)*   8. *(bed)*

C. Answers will vary.

D. tomato, tire, tie, tools, television or TV, toaster

Page 38

B. 1. s *(seed)*   2. s *(sandwich)*
    3. s *(six)*   4. s *(socks)*
    5. s *(saw)*   6. *(milk)*
    7. s *(safe)*   8. *(gate)*

C. Answers will vary.

D. seed, sandwich, six, socks, saw, safe

Page 39

B. 1. w *(watermelon)*   2. *(book)*
    3. w *(wallet)*   4. w *(watch)*
    5. w *(woman)*   6. w *(window)*
    7. *(feather)*   8. w *(web)*

C. Answers will vary.

D. watermelon, wallet, watch, woman, window, web

Page 40

A. 1. b *(robe)*   2. s *(glass)*
    3. s *(dress)*   4. b *(tub)*
    5. s *(gas)*   6. t *(bat)*
    7. t *(ant)*   8. t *(cat)*

B. 1. t   2. b   3. s   4. t
    5. yes   6. gas   7. set   8. job

Page 41

B. 1. o *(olive)*   2. *(tire)*
    3. *(ax)*   4. o *(otter)*
    5. o *(October)*   6. *(sick)*
    7. o *(ostrich)*   8. o *(ox)*

C. Answers will vary.

D. olive, otter, October, ostrich, ox

Page 42

B. 1. o *(bottle)*   2. o *(socks)*
    3. o *(cot)*   4. *(can)*
    5. o *(pot)*   6. o *(clock)*
    7. *(apple)*   8. o *(stop)*

C. Answers will vary.

D. bottle, socks, cot, pot, clock, stop

Page 43

A. 1. t *(tire)*   2. b *(belt)*
    3. w *(window)*   4. s *(sandwich)*
    5. o *(olive)*   6. b *(banana)*
    7. t *(television)*   8. w *(watch)*

B. 1. ox   2. pot   3. socks

Page 44

1. web   2. six   3. map   4. mop
5. box   6. ox   7. bat   8. gas
9. man   10. mat   11. ax   12. dam

Page 45

1. sat 2. Bob 3. got
4. Bob 5. smog 6. bad

Think About It

1. Bob sat at the dam.
2. Bob asked about the fog.
3. Smog is bad.

Page 46

B. bed, table, sick, water, web, cot, bus, olive, box

C. and D. Answers will vary.

Page 47

B. 1. k (kitchen) 2. (window)
   3. k (kettle) 4. k (kite)
   5. k (king) 6. (belt)
   7. k (key) 8. k (kitten)

C. Answers will vary.

D. kitchen, kettle, kite, king, key, kitten

Page 48

B. 1. (milk) 2. j (jam)
   3. j (jacket) 4. j (juice)
   5. j (jet) 6. j (jar)
   7. j (judge) 8. (banana)

C. Answers will vary

D. jam, jacket, juice, jet, jar, judge

Page 49

B. 1. p (pin) 2. (darts)
   3. p (pill) 4. (cot)
   5. p (parachute) 6. p (pencil)
   7. p (pot) 8. (football)

C. Answers will vary.

D. pin, pill, parachute, pencil, pot

Page 50

B. 1. n (newspaper) 2. (ax)
   3. (bat) 4. n (needle)
   5. n (note) 6. n (nail)
   7. n (net) 8. n (nest)

C. Answers will vary.

D. newspaper, needle, note, nail, net, nest

Page 51

A. 1. n (pan) 2. k (cake)
   3. p (tape) 4. n (kitten)
   5. k (bike) 6. p (cup)
   7. n (can) 8. k (rake)

B. 1. n 2. p 3. k 4. p
   5. map 6. bike 7. pin 8. jeep

Page 52

B. 1. i (igloo) 2. i (invitation)
   3. (apple) 4. i (ink)
   5. i (insulation) 6. (ox)
   7. i (inch) 8. (ax)

C. Answers will vary.

D. igloo, invitation, ink, insulation, inch

Page 53

B. 1. i (milk) 2. i (win)
   3. i (dishes) 4. (log)
   5. i (grill) 6. i (fish)
   7. (dam) 8. i (quilt)

C. Answers will vary.

D. milk, win, dishes, grill, fish, quilt

Page 54

A. 1. j (jacket) 2. k (kite)
   3. n (nail) 4. j (juice)
   5. p (pill) 6. i (invitation)
   7. k (key) 8. n (newspaper)

B. 1. win 2. sick 3. mitt

Page 55

1. pill   2. web   3. sick   4. gas
5. fan   6. desk   7. mitt   8. bed
9. pot   10. pin   11. jet   12. net

Page 56

1. at   2. big   3. pans
4. pats   5. hands   6. mops

Think About It

1. Don is at the sink.
2. Pots and pans are in the sink.
3. Pam mops by the sink.

Page 57

B. key, jeep, people, nurse, fork, mop, van, inch, mitt

C. and D. Answers will vary.

Page 58

B. 1. c (cap)   2. c (cake)
   3. c (cot)   4.   (otter)
   5. c (cub)   6. c (cup)
   7. c (cat)   8.   (table)

C. Answers will vary.

D. cap, cake, cot, cub, cup, cat

Page 59

B. 1. h (hat)   2. h (hive)
   3.   (king)   4. h (hole)
   5. h (hose)   6.   (pin)
   7. h (helmet)   8. h (hug)

C. Answers will vary.

D. hat, hive, hole, hose, helmet, hug

Page 60

B. 1.   (water)   2. l (ladder)
   3. l (log)   4. l (leaf)
   5. l (lock)   6.   (mop)
   7. l (letter)   8. l (lid)

C. Answers will vary.

D. ladder, log, leaf, lock, letter, lid

Page 61

B. 1. r (rake)   2. r (robe)
   3. r (rod)   4. r (rope)
   5.   (mat)   6. r (rose)
   7. r (rug)   8.   (helmet)

C. Answers will vary.

D. rake, robe, rod, rope, rose, rug

Page 62

B. 1. u (under)   2. u (umpire)
   3.   (inch)   4.   (ant)
   5. u (up)   6.   (rose)
   7.   (olive)   8. u (umbrella)

C. Answers will vary.

D. under, umpire, up, umbrella

Page 63

B. 1. u (tub)   2.   (cat)
   3. u (hug)   4. u (rug)
   5. u (gum)   6. u (cub)
   7.   (belt)   8. u (sun)

C. Answers will vary.

D. tub, hug, rug, gum, cub, sun

Page 64

A. 1. l (ladder)   2. h (helmet)
   3. u (umbrella) 4. r (rake)
   5. u (under)   6. r (radio)
   7. l (lid)   8. c (car)

B. 1. rug   2. sun   3. tub

Page 65

1. bus   2. car   3. sun   4. rug
5. can   6. gum   7. ham   8. cot
9. rod   10. belt   11. lid   12. cub

Page 66

1. got   2. run   3. as
4. hill   5. runs   6. cab

Think About It

1. Jud has a car that will not run.
2. He will get to his job in a cab.
3. The cab stops on the hill.

Page 67

B. car, home, light, radio, umbrella, cup

C. and D.   Answers will vary.

Page 68

B. 1.   (letter)   2. v (vase)
    3. v (vet)   4. v (vegetables)
    5. v (volcano)   6.   (wallet)
    7. v (van)   8. v (vine)

C. Answers will vary.

D. vase, vet, vegetables, volcano, van, vine

Page 69

B. 1. y (yellow)   2.   (can)
    3.   (robe)   4. y (yo-yo)
    5. y (yell)   6. y (yard)
    7. y (yield)   8. y (yarn)

C. Answers will vary.

D. yellow, yo-yo, yell, yard, yield, yarn

Page 70

B. 1. z (zipper)   2. z (zoo)
    3. z (zip code)   4.   (volcano)
    5. z (zebra)   6.   (pin)
    7. z (zero)   8.   (juice)

C. Answers will vary.

D. zipper, zoo, zip code, zebra, zero

Page 71

B. 1.   (zip code)   2. qu (quilt)
    3. qu (quarterback)   4. qu (queen)
    5.   (van)   6. qu (quarter)
    7.   (rod)   8. qu (quart)

C. Answers will vary.

D. quilt, quarterback, queen, quarter, quart

Page 72

B. 1. x (six)   2. x (fox)
    3. x (ax)   4.   (can)
    5. x (box)   6.   (food)
    7. x (wax)   8. x (tax)

C. Answers will vary.

D. six, fox, ax, box, wax, tax

Page 73

A. 1. l   2. x   3. l   4. v
    5. v   6. x   7. l   8. x

B. 1. x   2. v   3. l   4. v
    5. fi<u>v</u>e   6. ta<u>x</u>   7. mi<u>x</u>   8. unti<u>l</u>

Page 74

B. 1. e (engine)   2.   (umbrella)
    3. e (elephant)   4. e (elbow)
    5.   (flag)   6. e (exit)
    7.   (igloo)   8. e (elevator)

C. Answers will vary.

D. engine, elephant, elbow, exit, elevator

Page 75

B. 1. e (belt)   2.   (cat)
    3. e (net)   4. e (dress)
    5. e (vet)   6. e (men)
    7. e (nest)   8.   (bus)

C. Answers will vary

D. belt, net, dress, vet, men, nest

Page 76

A. 1. y *(yell)*   **2.** qu *(quilt)*
    3. v *(van)*   **4.** y *(yarn)*
    5. qu *(quarterback)*   **6.** z *(zip code)*
    7. z *(zoo)*   **8.** v *(volcano)*

B. 1. vet   **2.** bed   **3.** box

Page 77

1. hive   **2.** zip   **3.** men   **4.** six
5. ax   **6.** vet   **7.** box   **8.** queen
9. tub   **10.** yell   **11.** van   **12.** quilt

Page 78

1. band   **2.** can   **3.** quit
4. big   **5.** sing   **6.** fun

Think About It

1. Ben had a jazz band.
2. Ben quit the band because jazz can be sad.
3. Ben sings with a band.

Page 79

B. van, yell, zipper, quarter, ax, nail, five, egg, desk

C. and D. Answers will vary.

Page 80

    1. fan   **2.** dam   **3.** zip   **4.** cat
    5. quilt   **6.** box   **7.** gas   **8.** vet
    9. man   **10.** ham   **11.** dog   **12.** six

Page 81

1. bat   **2.** jet   **3.** cup   **4.** ax
    5. web   **6.** jam   **7.** yell   **8.** can
    9. bed   **10.** zoo   **11.** king   **12.** rug

Unit 3

Page 82

B. 1. a *(cake)*   **2.** *(box)*
    3. a *(gate)*   **4.** a *(safe)*
    5. *(inch)*   **6.** a *(game)*
    7. a *(rake)*   **8.** a *(cage)*

C. Answers will vary.

D. cake, gate, safe, game, rake, cage

Page 83

A. 1. fin   **2.** bat   **3.** cot

B. 1. cane   **2.** tape   **3.** mat
    4. man   **5.** cape   **6.** vane

Page 84

B. 1. *(bed)*   **2.** i *(dime)*
    3. i *(rice)*   **4.** i *(kite)*
    5. i *(dice)*   **6.** i *(pine)*
    7. i *(vine)*   **8.** i *(five)*

C. Answers will vary.

D. dime, rice, kite, dice, pine, vine, five

Page 85

A. 1. pin   **2.** dam   **3.** dog

B. 1. pill   **2.** kite   **3.** dime
    4. fin   **5.** win   **6.** file

Page 86

A. 1. a *(cane)*   **2.** i *(bike)*
    3. a *(cake)*   **4.** a *(safe)*
    5. i *(hive)*   **6.** i *(vine)*
    7. a *(cage)*   **8.** i *(rice)*

B. 1. rake   **2.** file   **3.** gate

Page 87

1. five   **2.** date   **3.** like
4. ride   **5.** lane   **6.** take

Think About It

1. It is ten past five.
2. Mike and Kate are going on a date.
3. They ride bikes to the lake.

Page 88

B. tape, kite, bike, cane, fine, cape

C. and D.   Answers will vary.

Page 89

B. 1. o *(hose)*   2. o *(tote)*
   3. o *(globe)*   4. o *(rope)*
   5. o *(smoke)*   6. o *(bone)*
   7. o *(hole)*   8. o *(stove)*

C. Answers will vary.

D. hose, tote, globe, rope, smoke, bone, hole, stove

Page 90

A. 1. lock   2. cot   3. pot

B. 1. mop   2. note   3. rod
   4. rope   5. tote   6. cone

Page 91

B. 1. u *(cube)*   2. u *(tube)*
   3. u *(fuse)*   4.   *(safe)*
   5. u *(June)*   6. u *(tune)*
   7.   *(dice)*   8. u *(flute)*

B. Answers will vary.

D. cube, tube, fuse, June, tune, flute

Page 92

A. 1. hug   2. bed   3. rug

B. 1. tube   2. cube   3. tune
   4. cub   5. fuse   6. cut

Page 93

A. 1. o *(bone)*   2. o *(rose)*
   3. u *(flute)*   4. u *(tube)*
   5. u *(June)*   6. o *(stove)*
   7. u *(mule)*   8. o *(rope)*

B. 1. cube   2. hose   3. hole

Page 94

1. home   2. robe   3. rose
4. nose   5. June   6. tune

Think About It

1. June is at home.
2. A rose is in the vase.
3. June hums as she makes lunch.

Page 95

B. robe, home, mule, hole, rode, tube

C. and D.   Answers will vary.

Page 96

B. 1. e *(jeans)*   2. e *(jeep)*
   3. e *(feet)*   4. e *(beet)*
   5. e *(seal)*   6. e *(teeth)*
   7. e *(weed)*   8. e *(tree)*

C. Answers will vary.

D. jeans, jeep, feet, beet, seal, teeth, weed, tree

Page 97

A. 1. jet   2. net   3. bed

B. 1. peas   2. team   3. sea
   4. beet   5. tea   6. meat

Page 98

1. beet   2. meat   3. tree
4. feet   5. jeep   6. bee
7. seal   8. weed   9. leaf

Page 99

1. team 2. week 3. meal
4. beef 5. meat 6. eat

Think About It

1. Jean is on a bike team.
2. This week they eat at Jean's home.
3. She grills lean beef and makes baked beans.

Page 100

B. leaf, bee, weed, eat, jeep, beans

C. and D. Answers will vary.

Page 102

Think About It

1. Sue is Joe's wife.
2. Dean has a big game at nine.
3. They want to get up at seven.
4. A pipe in the tub leaks.
5. Joe gets a pal to take them to the game.

Page 103

1. bone   2. cake   3. tube   4. vine
5. cone   6. cane   7. jeep   8. feet
9. note 10. weed 11. home 12. rice

Page 104

1. bike   2. five   3. rake   4. stove
5. cube   6. leaf   7. hose   8. safe
9. robe 10. fuse 11. kite 12. cape

Page 105

A. 1. hug   2. vane   3. gate   4. tax
    5. ant   6. meat   7. jam   8. six
    9. hole 10. nest 11. cap 12. jet

Page 106

B. 1. rod   2. bus   3. cube   4. pot
    5. dam   6. mail 7. zoo   8. bike
    9. win 10. bat 11. gum 12. cage

Page 107

C. 1. tub   2. file   3. men   4. hive
    5. yarn 6. fin   7. kite 8. web
    9. leaf 10. quart 11. bone 12. sun

Answer Key–Book One

Unit 1

Page 1

A. 1. <u>d</u>og   2. <u>b</u>ee   3. lea<u>f</u>   4. <u>c</u>at
    5. <u>f</u>ork   6. tu<u>b</u>   7. <u>c</u>up   8. food
    9. <u>c</u>ow   10. we<u>b</u>   11. <u>f</u>an   12. <u>d</u>oor

B. The first letter of each word must <u>b</u> or <u>c</u>.

C. The first letter of each word must be <u>d</u> or <u>f</u>.

Page 2

A. 1. rug   2. for<u>k</u>   3. <u>j</u>et   4. <u>h</u>ome
    5. <u>h</u>ug   6. <u>k</u>ey   7. gate   8. jar
    9. boo<u>k</u>   10. <u>h</u>at   11. <u>j</u>eep   12. gum

B. The first letter of each word must be g or <u>h</u>.

C. The first letter of each word must be <u>j</u> or <u>k</u>.

Page 3

A. 1. ca<u>n</u>   2. <u>l</u>ight   3. cap   4. <u>l</u>id
    5. <u>m</u>oney   6. cup   7. <u>n</u>urse   8. nai<u>l</u>
    9. ma<u>n</u>   10. <u>m</u>at   11. <u>l</u>og   12. pot

B. The first letter of each word must be <u>l</u> or <u>m</u>.

Page 4

A. 1. <u>s</u>ocks   2. car   3. ba<u>t</u>   4. <u>qu</u>ilt
    5. robe   6. <u>qu</u>arter 7. <u>s</u>ick   8. <u>t</u>ub
    9. <u>t</u>able   10. <u>r</u>ake   11. <u>qu</u>een 12. gas

B. The first letters of each word must be <u>qu</u> or <u>r</u>.

C. The first letter of each word must be <u>s</u> or <u>t</u>.

Page 5

A. 1. fo<u>x</u>   2. <u>z</u>ebra   3. <u>w</u>ater   4. <u>y</u>arn
    5. <u>w</u>atch   6. <u>v</u>ine   7. <u>w</u>eb   8. <u>z</u>ipper
    9. <u>y</u>oyo   10. <u>y</u>ard   11. bo<u>x</u>   12. <u>v</u>ase

B. The first letter of each word must be <u>v</u> or <u>w</u>.

C. The first letter of each word must be <u>x</u>, <u>y</u>, or <u>z</u>.

Unit 2

Page 6

A. 1. <u>a</u>pple   2. c<u>a</u>t   3. j<u>a</u>m   4. m<u>a</u>t
    5. c<u>a</u>p   6. p<u>a</u>n   7. c<u>a</u>n   8. <u>a</u>nt
    9. v<u>a</u>n   10. m<u>a</u>p   11. b<u>a</u>t   12. h<u>a</u>t

B. Each word must have short <u>a</u>.

Page 7

A. 1. t<u>ape</u>   2. c<u>ake</u>   3. r<u>ake</u>   4. c<u>age</u>
    5. g<u>ate</u>   6. s<u>afe</u>   7. c<u>ape</u>   8. v<u>ane</u>
    9. c<u>ane</u>   10. g<u>ame</u>   11. v<u>ase</u>   12. p<u>ane</u>

B. Each word must have long <u>a</u>.

Page 8

A. 1. tape   2. mat   3. cane
    4. man   5. cape   6. van
    7. hat   8. ace   9. pan

B. Discuss your sentence with your instructor.

C. Discuss your sentence with your instructor.

Page 9

A. 1. f<u>i</u>sh   2. d<u>i</u>shes   3. p<u>i</u>n   4. m<u>i</u>tt
    5. six   6. z<u>i</u>pper   7. s<u>i</u>ck   8. w<u>i</u>n
    9. <u>i</u>gloo   10. f<u>i</u>n   11. m<u>i</u>lk   12. p<u>i</u>ll

B. Each word have short <u>i</u>.

Page 10

A. 1. b<u>ike</u>   2. p<u>ine</u>   3. v<u>ine</u>   4. k<u>ite</u>
    5. h<u>ive</u>   6. d<u>ice</u>   7. f<u>ile</u>   8. r<u>ice</u>
    9. f<u>ive</u>   10. d<u>ime</u>   11. m<u>ice</u>   12. r<u>ide</u>

B. Each word must have long <u>i</u>.

Page 11

A. 1. pine   2. pill   3. kite
    4. win   5. file   6. fin
    7. dime   8. time   9. ride

B. Discuss your sentence with your instructor.

C. Discuss your sentence with your instructor.

Page 12

A. 1. kite   2. pine   3. hive
     4. came   5. race   6. time

B. 1. They flew a kite.
     2. It hit a bee hive.
     3. No, the bees did not get them.

Page 13

A. 1. s<u>o</u>cks   2. p<u>o</u>t   3. f<u>o</u>x   4. l<u>o</u>ck
     5. <u>o</u>live   6. <u>o</u>x   7. m<u>o</u>p   8. b<u>o</u>x
     9. c<u>o</u>t   10. l<u>o</u>g   11. r<u>o</u>d   12. cl<u>o</u>ck

B. Each word must have short <u>o</u>.

Page 14

A. 1. r<u>obe</u>   2. h<u>ole</u>   3. b<u>one</u>   4. n<u>ote</u>
     5. h<u>ose</u>   6. c<u>one</u>   7. st<u>ove</u>   8. r<u>ose</u>
     9. sm<u>oke</u> 10. r<u>ope</u>   11. h<u>ome</u> 12. t<u>ote</u>

B. Each word must have long <u>o</u>.

Page 15

A. 1. robe   2. mop   3. cone
     4. rope   5. dog   6. tote
     7. lock   8. rod   9. note

B. Discuss your sentence with your instructor.

C. Discuss your sentence with your instructor.

Page 16

A. 1. r<u>ug</u>   2. t<u>ub</u>   3. s<u>un</u>   4. g<u>um</u>
     5. b<u>us</u>   6. c<u>up</u>   7. c<u>ub</u>   8. h<u>ug</u>
     9. <u>u</u>mbrella 10. judge 11. <u>u</u>mpire 12. <u>u</u>p

B. Each word must have short <u>u</u>.

Page 17

A. 1. m<u>u</u>le   2. c<u>u</u>be   3. f<u>use</u>
     4. t<u>u</u>be   5. J<u>u</u>ne   6. fl<u>u</u>te
     7. t<u>u</u>ne   8. r<u>u</u>ler   9. f<u>u</u>mes

B. Each word must have long <u>u</u>.

Page 18

A. 1. tube   2. cub   3. fuse
     4. tub   5. cube   6. hug
     7. tune   8. mule   9. cut

B. Discuss your sentence with your instructor.

C. Discuss your sentence with your instructor.

Page 19

1. mule   2. nose   3. home
4. fuse   5. hole   6. bone

Page 20

A. 1. d<u>e</u>sk   2. <u>e</u>gg   3. w<u>e</u>b   4. p<u>e</u>n
     5. t<u>e</u>n   6. p<u>e</u>t   7. n<u>e</u>t   8. h<u>e</u>n
     9. j<u>e</u>t   10. b<u>e</u>d   11. l<u>e</u>g   12. b<u>e</u>ll

B. Each word must have short <u>e</u>.

Page 21

A. 1. l<u>ea</u>f   2. b<u>ee</u>   3. j<u>ee</u>p   4. s<u>ea</u>l
     5. f<u>ee</u>t   6. m<u>ea</u>t   7. w<u>ee</u>ds   8. t<u>ea</u>
     9. s<u>ea</u>   10. s<u>ee</u>d   11. qu<u>ee</u>n 12. t<u>ea</u>m

B. Each word must have long <u>ea</u>.

C. Each word must have long <u>ee</u>.

Page 22

A. 1. men   2. seal   3. weed
     4. bed   5. meat   6. net
     7. tea   8. leaf   9. beet

B. Discuss your sentence with your instructor.

C. Discuss your sentence with your instructor.

Page 23

A. 1. Ted   2. rode   3. seats
     4. eat   5. cone   6. team

B. 1. They rode the bus.
   2. They ate a hot dog and an ice-cream cone.
   3. The Red Sox won.
   4. Discuss your answer with your teacher.

Unit 3

Page 24

C. It is the end of the big race.
   A man and a woman stand.
   A boy and a girl sit.
   Two people run to win the race.
   Who will win the race?

Page 25

B. 1. big, big   2. run, run
   3. sit, sit   4. man, man
   5. stand, stand

C. 1. man   2. sit
   3. stand   4. run
   5. big

Page 26

C. A man and a woman stop at the store.
   They go into the store.
   He buys a can of cat food.
   She buys some food for lunch.
   They stand next to a table.

Page 27

B. 1. can, can   2. table, table
   3. stop, stop   4. go, go
   5. food, food

C. 1. can   2. food
   3. table   4. stop
   5. go

D. 1–5 Discuss your sentences with your instructor.

Page 28

A. 1. runs, runs   2. goes, goes
   3. sits, sits   4. does, does
   5. stands, stands   6. watches, watches
   7. stops, stops   8. fixes, fixes

B. 1. A man runs.

Page 29

C. 1. goes   2. stops   3. fixes
   4. watches 5. sits   6. does

D. 1. runs   2. fixes   3. goes
   4. stands   5. sits   6. watches

Page 30

A. 1. stand   2. sit   3. table   4. run

B. 1. A man sits.   2. A man stops.
   3. The man is big.

Page 31

B. 4. A woman can lift.
   5. A man fixes.
   6. A girl does homework.

C. 3. The woman watches.

D. 1. does, does   2. stops, stops
   3. fixes, fixes   4. stands, stands

Page 32

C. The woman is home from her job.
   She will use her key to open the door.
   She waves at a friend.
   He is going for a walk.

Page 33

B. 1. home, home   2. walk, walk
   3. key, key   4. use, use
   5. woman, woman

C. 1. key   2. woman 3. home
   4. walk   5. use

D. 1–5 Discuss your sentences with your instructor.

Page 34

C. The woman has some money.
She wants to buy the radio.
The man has to yell at his dog.
He tells the dog to stop barking.

Page 35

B. 1. yell, yell   2. dog, dog
3. radio, radio   4. buy, buy
5. money, money

C. 1. dog   2. money   3. yell
4. radio   5. buy

Page 36

A. 1. homes, homes   2. ranches, ranches
3. keys, keys   4. grasses, grasses
5. dogs, dogs   6. bosses, bosses
7. tables, tables   8. boxes, boxes
9. radios, radios

B. 3. The woman buys tables.

Page 37

C. 1. bosses   2. keys   3. grass   4. dogs
5. homes   6. radios   7. boxes   8. tables

Page 38

A. 1. money   2. woman   3. yells   4. uses

B. 1. A man buys radios.
2. The dogs sit.
3. A woman uses keys.

Page 39

B. 4. The man yells.
5. The boys sit on the grass.
6. The woman carries boxes.

C. 2. The woman walks the dogs.

Page 40

C. The car is on the country road.
The man is starting to work on it.
His brother and sister watch him work.
They want to go for a ride.

Page 41

B. 1. brother, brother   2. car, car
3. sister, sister   4. work, work
5. country, country

C. 1. work   2. country   3. car
4. brother   5. sister

D. 1-5 Discuss your sentences with your instructor.

Page 42

C. The family is washing the van. Dad sprays on the water. Mom washes the van with the soap. The son will help dry the van. His little sisters play in the van. They look out the window.

Page 43

B. 1. family, family   2. look, look
3. van, van   4. water, water
5. help, help

C. 1. family   2. look   3. van
4. water   5. help

D. 1–5 Discuss your sentences with your instructor.

Page 44

A. 1. worked, worked   2. helped, helped
3. looked, looked   4. yelled, yelled
5. walked, walked

B. 1. The people worked.

Page 45

C. 1. walked 2. worked 3. helped
   4. yelled 5. looked

D. 1. The brother yelled.
   2. He helped fix the pipe.
   3. The woman worked.

Page 46

A. 1. country 2. van
   3. go 4. water

B. 1. The sister worked.
   2. The brother helped.
   3. The family looked.

Page 47

4. The family walked.
5. The sister yelled.
6. The brother worked.

C. 1. helped 2. woman
   3. food 4. brother

Page 48

C. The man in bed is sick. The nurse takes
   care of him. A friend brings a plant to wish
   him well. The man hopes he will get to go
   home soon.

Page 49

B. 1. sick 2. nurse 3. well
   4. bed 5. get

C. 1. bed 2. well 3. sick
   4. nurse 5. get

D. Discuss your sentence with your instructor.

Page 50

C. Here is a busy street in the city. A man
   runs from the store. He would like to get
   the bus. He would like to get a seat on the
   bus. A woman will pay for a paper.

Page 51

B. 1. like 2. pay 3. store
   4. bus 5. city

C. 1. store 2. bus 3. like
   4. pay 5. city

D. Discuss your sentence with your instructor.

Page 52

C. These people need help from the boss. They
   are learning a new job. The boss is telling
   them how to pay the bills. They are looking
   at the bills to pay this month. The light helps
   them see well.

Page 53

B. 1. bills, bills 2. boss, boss
   3. people, people 4. job, job
   5. light, light

C. 1. light 2. boss 3. bills
   4. job 5. people

D. 1-5 Discuss your sentences with your
   instructor.

Page 54

A. 1. walking, walking 2. paying, paying
   3. looking, looking 4. helping, helping
   5. yelling, yelling 6. working, working
   7. going, going 8. doing, doing

B. 2. the people yelling

Page 55

C. 1. going 2. paying 3. looking

D. 1. walking 2. working 3. looking
   4. paying 5. helping 6. yelling

Page 56

A. 1. pay 2. sick
   3. gets 4. bus

B. **1.** a man buying food
2. the boss paying
3. a woman walking

Page 57

C. **1.** bed **2.** job **3.** store
4. bus **5.** city **6.** boss
7. people **8.** well **9.** likes

D. **1.** work<u>ing</u>, working **2.** help<u>ing</u>, helping
3. go<u>ing</u>, going **4.** yell<u>ing</u>, yelling
5. look<u>ing</u>, looking **6.** pay<u>ing</u>, paying
7. walk<u>ing</u>, walking

Page 58

A. **1.** st<u>o</u>p **2.** cit<u>y</u> **3.** lik<u>e</u> **4.** w<u>e</u>ll
5. <u>c</u>ar **6.** pe<u>o</u>ple **7.** b<u>i</u>lls **8.** w<u>a</u>lk
9. job **10.** l<u>i</u>ght **11.** h<u>o</u>me **12.** <u>n</u>urse

B. **1.** woman **2.** sick **3.** bed
4. man **5.** yells **6.** van

Page 59

C. **1.** pay<u>s</u>, pays **2.** work<u>s</u>, works
3. do<u>es</u>, does **4.** watch<u>es</u>, watches
5. stop<u>s</u>, stops **6.** run<u>s</u>, runs
7. fix<u>es</u>, fixes **8.** sit<u>s</u>, sits
9. walk<u>s</u>, walks **10.** go<u>es</u>, goes

D. **1.** help<u>ed</u>, helped **2.** yell<u>ed</u>, yelled
3. look<u>ed</u>, looked **4.** walk<u>ed</u>, walked
5. work<u>ed</u>, worked **6.** fix<u>ed</u>, fixed

E. **1.** look<u>ing</u>, looking **2.** work<u>ing</u>, working
3. go<u>ing</u>, going **4.** pay<u>ing</u>, paying
5. help<u>ing</u>, helping **6.** walk<u>ing</u>, walking
7. do<u>ing</u>, doing **8.** yell<u>ing</u>, yelling

Unit 4

Page 60

B. **1.** an apple **2.** an egg
3. an umbrella

Page 61

B. **1.** She; He; She, and, he
2. He; She; He, and, she
3. He; She; He, and, she

Page 62

B. **1.** is; was; were **2.** was; is; are
3. are; was; is

Page 63

B. **1.** You, I **2.** I
3. They **4.** You, I
5. They

Page 64

B. **1.** This; it **2.** This; That
3. this, that **4.** that, it
5. this, that

Page 65

1. He **2.** They **3.** the
4. and **5.** is **6.** was

Page 66

B. **1.** was; She **2.** He; She; They
3. a; It; I **4.** Are; Is; You
5. the; and; That

C. I can use <u>this</u> van. He <u>and</u> she can use <u>the</u> car. <u>You</u> can use <u>the</u> bus. They are walking to <u>the</u> car.

Page 67

A. **1.** You, are; She, is
2. You, are; He, is; You, he, are

B. **2.** You are going home. He is going home. He and you are going home.

Page 68

A. 1. They, are; That, is
   2. They, were; That, is; That, is
B. 2. That is the money. That is the light bill.
      They are paying the light bill.

Page 69

A. 1. This, is; This, is; She, and, I
   2. This, is; This, is; She, and, I
B. 2. She and I buy the food. This is the food
      the family likes.

Page 70

A. 1. The, was; It, was, a
   2. The; The
   3. The; They, were
B. 2. The people were standing. The cars
      were going.

Page 71

A. 1. This, was, that, was
   2. This, was, that, was
   3. This, was, that, was
B. 1. That was a home. This was a home.

Page 72

1. This is; It was   2. That is; She and I
3. a; He is   4. the; They are

Page 73

B. 1. You are; This is
   2. He is; She and I
   3. a; It was
   4. That is; They are; the
   5. He is; a
C. That is the light bill. She and I are paying it.
   That is the food bill. They are paying that
   bill. You can help pay the bills.

Page 74

A. 1. Who, with   2. for
   3. has   4. Who, with, us
B. 1. The brother walks with us.
      He has a sister.
      The sister walks with us.
      She has a radio.
   2. The man sits with us.
      He has a dog.
      The woman sits with us.
      She walks with us.
   3. The dog has a home.
      He sits for us.
      He runs with us.
      He likes us.
   4. Who works with us?
      Who works for money?
      The boss has money.
      The boss pays us for working.

Page 75

A. 1. Why, does, him   2. Why, her
   3. Why, does, them   4. Why, does, to
B. 1. The man helps her.
      The woman helps him.
   2. He walks to work with her.
      She walks to work with him.
      They go to work with them.
   3. This woman walks to work.
      She likes her job.
      The boss pays her well.
      Why does she like her boss?
      She likes working for her.
   4. She buys food for them.
      Does she buy it for him?

Page 76

A. 1. me   2. by, me
    3. from   4. When, we

B. 1. Get the money <u>from</u> <u>me</u>.
<u>When</u> can you go for me?
The money is <u>by</u> the bed.
You can go to the store for <u>me</u>.

    2. He works with <u>me</u>.
He and I get money <u>by</u> working.
We get the money <u>from</u> the boss.
<u>When</u> can <u>we</u> get the money?

    3. He can go home <u>from</u> work.
He can walk with <u>me</u> to the bus stop.
<u>We</u> stand <u>by</u> the bus stop.

    4. <u>We</u> walk <u>by</u> the store.
<u>We</u> get food <u>from</u> the store.
The food is for you and <u>me</u>.
<u>We</u> like the food store.

Page 77

A. 1. am, at; not, at   2. am; not
    3. cannot; cannot   4. have; at

B. 1. I <u>have</u> a home.
I <u>am</u> going home.
I <u>am</u> <u>not</u> <u>at</u> work.

    2. I <u>have</u> bills to pay.
I <u>have</u> money to pay them.
I <u>am</u> paying the bills.

    3. I <u>am</u> going to work.
I <u>cannot</u> walk to work.
I <u>am</u> standing at the bus stop.

    4. I <u>am</u> <u>at</u> the store.
I <u>cannot</u> buy a radio.
I <u>have</u> bills to pay.

Page 78

A. 1. no; Where   2. Where; in
    3. Both, of   4. Both, of

B. 1. We are <u>in</u> the store.
<u>Both</u> <u>of</u> us have money.
He has <u>no</u> money.

    2. <u>Both</u> <u>of</u> us like the country.
We have <u>no</u> work <u>in</u> the country.
<u>Both</u> <u>of</u> us work <u>in</u> the city.

    3. <u>Both</u> <u>of</u> us have cars.
<u>Where</u> can we go?
<u>Both</u> <u>of</u> us go to the city.

    4. <u>Both</u> <u>of</u> us have quarters.
<u>Both</u> <u>of</u> us use the quarters.
<u>Where</u> is the food?

Page 79

    1. at; with   2. of; Both
    3. no; has   4. cannot; Does

Page 80

B. 1. am; us   2. has; by
    3. her; with   4. in; We; us

C. Her family helps <u>at</u> home. The brother gets money for helping with the work. He gets money from the sisters. Both of <u>them</u> pay <u>him</u> <u>to</u> work.

The sisters <u>have</u> jobs at the food store. They are <u>not</u> at home. <u>Both</u> <u>of</u> <u>them</u> <u>have</u> cars to get to work.

The brother has <u>no</u> car. He uses the bus. He pays <u>for</u> the bus <u>with</u> the money he gets <u>from</u> the sisters.

Page 81

A. 1. am, at; am; am
    2. am; from, him; from, him
    3. am, him; am, from; am, at, him

B. 2. She is looking at him. He is looking at her.

123

Page 82

A. 1. by   2. Both, of, them
     3. Both, of, them   4. Both
     5. Both, of, them, by

B. 1. People get bills, and people pay them.

Page 83

A. 1. We, cannot; We, not, we
     2. with, us; not, with, us
     3. We, with; cannot, with, us

B. 2. She is not going with us. She is going to work in her car.

Page 84

A. 1. have, no; has, in; in; has
     2. No, in; have; has

B. 1. The dog has her food. I have water for her.

Page 85

A. 1. for, her; me, to, her
     2. for, me, to; for, her, to
     3. to, for, me; her, for, her

B. 2. She uses her money to buy food. The food is for her family.

Page 86

     1. Both; cannot; We   2. by; am; to
     3. have; at; Her   4. has; at; for

Page 87

B. 1. We; us; not   2. have; at; am
     3. from; me; by

C. This man and I work in the city. <u>Both</u> <u>of</u> <u>us</u> walk home <u>from</u> work.

We stop <u>by</u> the home of a sick family. The man <u>has</u> food <u>for</u> <u>them</u>. He pays the bills <u>for</u> <u>them</u>.

The family likes <u>him</u>. He is like a brother to the people <u>in</u> <u>this</u> family. He has <u>no</u> family <u>in</u> <u>this</u> city.

Page 88

A. 1. so   2. very   3. your   4. very

B. 1. The light is <u>so</u> bright. The light is <u>very</u> bright.

     2. Is <u>your</u> street very long? My street is <u>so</u> long I can't see the end. It is a <u>very</u> quiet street.

     3. I love my dog <u>so</u> much. Is <u>your</u> dog <u>very</u> small? I like <u>very</u> small dogs.

     4. Is she <u>your</u> teacher? The teacher is <u>very</u> nice. I am <u>so</u> glad she is my teacher.

Page 89

A. 1. Would, ask   2. been
     3. ask   4. Ask, if, been

B. 1. Where has she <u>been</u>? I wonder <u>if</u> she has <u>been</u> to school. <u>Would</u> you <u>ask</u> her?

     2. He has <u>been</u> sick. He will get well <u>if</u> he stays in bed.

     3. I have not <u>been</u> to the park. <u>Would</u> she like to go to the park? I <u>would</u> like for her to come. I will <u>ask</u> her.

     4. She has <u>been</u> at work. She will have fun <u>if</u> she comes.

Page 90

A. 1. up, their   2. Yes
     3. Yes, their   4. up

B. 1. Their house is <u>up</u> the hill. <u>Yes</u>, it is very high. They must climb <u>up</u> the hill every day.

     2. They asked her to <u>their</u> party. She said <u>yes</u>.

3. The stairs go <u>up</u> to the sixth floor.
<u>Their</u> office is on the third floor.

4. <u>Their</u> plane will land soon. Can you see it <u>up</u> in the sky? <u>Yes</u>, I can see it.

Page 91

1. your, Yes   **2.** been, very
3. if, would   **4.** so, up

Page 92

A. **1.** Your, so; your; your; very
2. so; very; your
3. Your, very; your; Your, so

B. **3.** He is very happy. She is very happy, too.

Page 93

A. **1.** ask, if, been; been; would, if
2. would, if; been; ask
3. If, would; ask; if

B. **1.** The man has not been to the store.
The man has been to the store.

Page 94

A. **1.** Their, up; Yes, up; their
2. up, yes; Their
3. up, up, Their

B. **2.** Their cat is up in a tree. Yes, I will go get it.

Page 95

A. **1.** Would, yes   **2.** been, asks
3. your, their   **4.** Would, If

Page 96

A. zero   <u>one</u> home   <u>two</u> beds
<u>three</u> tables   <u>four</u> people   <u>five</u> lights

B. 0   five
1   zero
2   four

3   one
4   two
5   three

C. zero   one   two   three   our   five

Page 97

A. <u>six</u> radios   <u>seven</u> keys   <u>eight</u> bills
<u>nine</u> quarters   <u>ten</u> zippers

B. 6   eight
7   nine
8   seven
9   ten
10   six

C. six   seven   eight   nine   ten

Page 98

A. eight—8   seven—7   one—1
nine—9   five—5   six—6
two—2   zero—0   four—4
three—3   ten—10

B. 3—three   6—six   0—zero
5—five   2—two   7—seven
1—one   4—four   8—eight
9—nine   10—ten

C. 5—five   3—three   7—seven
1—one   10—ten   4—four
8—eight   0—zero   6—six
9—nine   10—ten   2—two

Page 99

A. zero, one, two, three, four, five, six, seven, eight, nine, ten

B. The Family

The family has <u>two</u> brothers and <u>three</u> sisters. The family has <u>five</u> people in it. The family has <u>one</u> home. The home has lights, tables, beds, and radios. <u>One</u> of the lights is by a table, and <u>two</u> of them are not. The home has <u>three</u> lights.

Four of the family work at a food store. Six people work with the family at the store. <u>Ten</u> people work at the store. Eight of the people at the store are well, and <u>two</u> people are sick.

Page 100

A. 1. five; circle around first butterfly
   2. ten; circle around sixth spoon
   3. four; circle around third box
   4. nine; one; circle around eighth banana

Page 101

B. 1. three, first
   2. five, fifth
   3. four, fourth
   4. two, second
   5. five, fourth
   6. six, sixth
   7. ten, tenth
   8. nine, seventh
   9. nine, first

Page 102

A. 1. <u>c</u>an, <u>c</u>up, <u>c</u>ap, <u>c</u>ake, <u>c</u>one
   2. <u>f</u>ork, <u>f</u>amily, <u>f</u>rom, <u>f</u>or, <u>f</u>ish
   3. <u>m</u>oney, <u>m</u>at, <u>m</u>ice, <u>m</u>ule, <u>m</u>an
   4. <u>r</u>adio, <u>r</u>obe, <u>r</u>ake, <u>r</u>ide, <u>r</u>ose

B. Answers will vary. Rhymes for:
   1. bin, 2. bat, 3. can, 4. fox

C. Answers will vary. Word with the same first letter as: 1. bed, 2. can, 3. dog, 4. food, 5. light, 6. nurse, 7. sister, 8. work

Page 103

D. 1. walking, very, stops
   2. Would, She and I, food
   3. country, family, can
   4. their, table, This is
   5. nurse, bed, well
   6. store, money, keys

Page 104

E. 1. job<u>s</u>, jobs
   2. stand<u>ing</u>, standing
   3. radio<u>s</u>, radios
   4. walk<u>ed</u>, walked
   5. key<u>s</u>, keys
   6. go<u>ing</u>, going
   7. help<u>ed</u>, helped
   8. watch<u>es</u> *or* watch<u>ed</u>, watches or watched
   9. look<u>ing</u>, looking
   10. work<u>ed</u>, worked
   11. yell<u>s</u>, yells
   12. help<u>ing</u>, helping

F. 1. fifth   2. eighth   3. second
   4. tenth   5. ten

Page 106

<u>Think About It</u>

1. Pam's brother was sick.
2. She rides a bus to get to her job.
3. She stops by to help him because he is sick.
4. He will go to work today.

Blackline Masters

The blackline masters on pages 128–137 provide practice or enrichment for material the *Reading for Today* student books. You may duplicate as many copies as you need for classroom use. Each blackline master is referenced in the Instructor Notes in the student book where it seems most useful. However, the blackline masters can be used with any book and in any way you think would be helpful for your students.

Blackline Master 1: Writing Practice Lines

This page consists of writing lines for beginning writers. Each line contains a dotted mid-point line as well as a base line and top line to help students form letters correctly. Use this page to provide students in the Introductory Book and Book One with writing paper for extra practice in writing letters, numbers, words, and sentences.

Blackline Master 2: Alphabet Review

This page provides a review of the upper and lower case letters of the alphabet and visual discrimination of letters. Use it at the beginning of Book One as a review or as a way to determine the students' readiness to work in Book One. If students cannot complete this page successfully, they should begin with the Introductory Book. The page may also be used for extra practice with Unit 1 of the Introductory Book.

Blackline Master 3a and 3b: Phonics Word List

This list contains example words for all the consonant, short vowel, and long vowel sounds taught in Book One. Use parts or all of this list to reinforce the phonics skills covered in Book One. The list may also provide words to make flash cards or word games to reinforce phonics skills.

Blackline Master 4: The 5Ws Checklist

This is a comprehension checklist built around the traditional *who, what, when, where, why,* and *how* scheme commonly referred to as the 5Ws even though *how* is usually included as well. This page provides an easy-to-use way to enhance student comprehension of the stories in the student books. It can be used with all the stories in all the books. Have students keep their completed checklists for each story in their journals or notebooks.

Blackline Master 5a and 5b: Survival Words

These two pages contain an alphabetical list of words that adults commonly encounter in their everyday lives. Use the list to help students learn these words as sight words. Work on a small group of words at a time until students can read them without hesitation. Then move on to another group of words. You may also use these words to make flash cards or as a word bank for students to dictate or write their own sentences. The list can be used beginning with the Introductory Book and continuing through all the student books or in any way that fits your students and their needs.

Blackline Master 6: Useful Abbreviations

This list of common abbreviations supplements the lessons in Book Four on writing abbreviations. It can also be used as in later books as a review and reference for abbreviations.

Blackline Master 7: World Map

This outline map of the world is designed to be used with the story in Unit 3 of Book Five. Specific suggestions are included in the Instructor Notes on those pages of the student book.

Blackline Master 8: Certificate of Completion

This certificate provides a way to recognize students' achievement in successfully completing each book in the *Reading for Today* program.

Blackline Master 1: Writing Practice Lines

Alphabet Review

A. Write the missing letters.

__B__ __ __F__ __ __J__ __ __N

O__ __ __ __ __U__ __ __Y__

B. Write the missing letters.

a__ __ __e__ __ __i__ __ __m

n__ __q__ __ __t__ __ __x__ __ __

C. Circle the same letter.

1. m	m	r	m	n	m	m	h	m
2. F	E	L	F	F	E	F	H	E
3. b	h	b	p	b	b	d	b	q
4. O	O	Q	O	C	O	D	O	Q
5. g	g	g	d	p	g	q	g	b
6. U	V	W	U	U	V	U	U	V

Phonics Word List

Consonants

b (initial)
back
be
bee
belt
boy

b (final)
club
cub
grab
job
tub

c (initial)
cage
can
car
cat
catch

d (initial)
day
dish
dog
dollar
door

d (final)
did
good
lad
odd
said

f (initial)
fast
few
five
fix
food
four

f (final)
half
if
leaf
myself
wolf

g (initial)
gas
gate
gift
girl
go
got
gun

g (final)
big
dog
flag
frog
log

h (initial)
happy
has
hat
have
he
help

j (initial)
jacket
jar
joke
July
jump
just

k (initial)
keep
kick
kid
kiss
kite

k (final)
bike
book
cook
like
look
make

l (initial)
leak
left
letter
lift
like
list

l (final)
all
bill
shall
small
spell
vowel

m (initial)
make
man
many
me

men
money
must

m (final)
aim
from
him
room
them

n (initial)
no
nose
nest
next
now

n (final)
can
pen
rain
then
when

p (initial)
penny
people
picnic
pig
pocket
pull

p (final)
cap
sleep
step
stop
up

qu (initial)
quart
quarter
quick
quiet
quiz

r (initial)
radio
rest
ride
rock
room

s (initial)
same
say
see
sell
soft

s (final)
bus
cactus
gas
its
plus
this
us
yes

t (initial)
table
take
talk
teach
ticket
today

t (final)
bat
coat
hat
put
wait
want

v (initial)
van
vegetable
vet
very
visit
volcano
vote

v (final)
above
five
give
have
wave

w (initial)
walk
was
we
will
with
woman

x (final)
fix
fox
mix
ox
relax
six
tax
wax

y (initial)
year
yell
yellow
yes
you

z (initial)
zebra
zero
zigzag
zip
zone
zoo

Short Vowels

a (initial)
am
an
animal
apple
as
ask
at
ax

a (medial)
bat
fan
jazz
lap
man
mat
nap
pan
pat
tan

-ab
cab
dab
gab
jab
tab

-ad
bad
dad
had
mad
pad
sad

-ag
bag
gag
nag
rag

sag
tag
wag

-am
dam
ham
jam
Pam
Sam
yam

-and
and
band
hand
land
sand

e (initial)
egg
elevator
empty
enter
exercise
exit

e (medial)
bell
fell
leg
less
men
mess
tell
ten
web
well

-ed
bed
fed
led
Ned
red
Ted
wed

-end
bend
end
fend
lend
mend
send
tend

-ent
bent

cent
dent
Kent
lent
rent
sent
tent
went

-et
bet
get
jet
let
met
net
pet
set
wet
yet

i (medial)
did
dig
dip
fill
hill
him
hip
lid
miss
rip
tip
wig
will
zip

-in
fin
gin
kin
pin
tin
win

-it
bit
fit
hit
kit
pit
quit
sit
wit

o (initial)
October
on

open
operator
ox

o (medial)
boss
box
doll
job
nod
rob
sob

-op
cop
hop
mop
pop
top

-ot
cot
dot
got
hot
lot
not
pot
rot

u (initial)
umbrella
uncle
under
up
us

u (medial)
bud
bus
dull
gum
hug
hum
mud
rub
rug
sum
tub

-un
bun
fun
gun
nun
run
sun

-ut
but
cut
gut
hut
jut
nut
rut

Long Vowels

a_e
cake
came
cape
cave
date
game
lake
lane
male
name
pane
rake
safe
sale
same
save
tale
tame
wade
wake

ea
bead
beak
beam
bean
eat
heal
heat
lean
leap
meat
neat
read
sea
seat
tea
team
weak

ee
deep
eel
feed
feel

feet
meet
need
peek
queen
seed
seek
seem
seen
weed
week
weep

i_e
dime
fine
hide
line
mice
mine
nice
nine
pine
rice
ride
side
time
wide
wine

o_e
bone
cone
cope
hole
home
hope
mope
note
pole
robe
rode
rope
tone
vote
woke

u_e
cube
cute
due
June
rude
rule
tube
tune
use

The 5Ws Checklist

___ Who   ___ When
___ What   ___ Where
___ Why + ___ How

WHO is the story about?

_____

_____

_____

WHAT happens in the story?

_____

_____

_____

_____

WHY do the people in the story do what they do?

_____

_____

_____

WHEN and WHERE does the story happen?

_____

_____

_____

HOW does the story end?

_____

_____

_____

Survival Words

A

admission	ADMISSION
airport	AIRPORT

B

bank	BANK
beware of dog	BEWARE OF DOG
bus stop	BUS STOP

C

cashier	CASHIER
caution	CAUTION
clinic	CLINIC
closed	CLOSED
crosswalk	CROSSWALK

D

danger	DANGER
dead end	DEAD END
detour	DETOUR
do not enter	DO NOT ENTER
don't walk	DON'T WALK
down	DOWN

E

elevator	ELEVATOR
emergency room	EMERGENCY ROOM
employees only	EMPLOYEES ONLY
entrance	ENTRANCE
enter	ENTER
exit	EXIT
explosives	EXPLOSIVES
express checkout	EXPRESS CHECKOUT

F

fire department	FIRE DEPARTMENT
fire escape	FIRE ESCAPE
fire exit	FIRE EXIT
fire extinguisher	FIRE EXTINGUISHER
first aid	FIRST AID
flammable	FLAMMABLE

for rent	FOR RENT
for sale	FOR SALE

H

handicapped	HANDICAPPED
hazard	HAZARD
hazardous waste	HAZARDOUS WASTE
help wanted	HELP WANTED
high voltage	HIGH VOLTAGE
hospital	HOSPITAL

I

information	INFORMATION

K

keep away	KEEP AWAY
keep out	KEEP OUT

L

left	LEFT
left turn only	LEFT TURN ONLY
library	LIBRARY
loading zone	LOADING ZONE

M

men	MEN

N

no admittance	NO ADMITTANCE
no left turn	NO LEFT TURN
no parking	NO PARKING
no smoking	NO SMOKING
no trespassing	NO TRESPASSING
no vacancy	NO VACANCY

O

office	OFFICE
one way	ONE WAY
open	OPEN
out of order	OUT OF ORDER

P

park	PARK
pedestrians	PEDESTRIANS
ped xing	PED XING
pharmacy	PHARMACY
phone	PHONE
police station	POLICE STATION
poison	POISON
post office	POST OFFICE
private	PRIVATE
private property	PRIVATE PROPERTY
prohibited	PROHIBITED
public transportation	PUBLIC TRANSPORTATION
pull	PULL
push	PUSH

R

railroad crossing	RAILROAD CROSSING
reserved	RESERVED
rest rooms	REST ROOMS
right	RIGHT
restricted area	RESTRICTED AREA

S

school	SCHOOL
school zone	SCHOOL ZONE
self service	SELF SERVICE
slow	SLOW
speed limit	SPEED LIMIT
stop	STOP
subway	SUBWAY

T

taxi	TAXI
toll lane	TOLL LANE

U

up	UP
use other door	USE OTHER DOOR

V

vacancy	VACANCY

Y

yield	YIELD

W

waiting room	WAITING ROOM
walk	WALK
warning	WARNING
watch your step	WATCH YOUR STEP
women	WOMEN
wrong way	WRONG WAY

Useful Abbreviations

CALENDAR

Sun.	Sunday
Mon.	Monday
Tues.	Tuesday
Wed.	Wednesday
Thurs.	Thursday
Fri.	Friday
Sat.	Saturday
Jan.	January
Feb.	February
Mar.	March
Apr.	April
Aug.	August
Sept.	September
Oct.	October
Nov.	November
Dec.	December

MEASUREMENT

c/C	cup
cm	centimeter
doz.	dozen
ft.	foot/feet
g	gram
gal	gallon
in.	inch
km	kilometer
L/l	liter
lb.	pound
m	meter
oz.	ounce
pt.	pint
qt.	quart
tbsp/T	tablespoon
tsp/t	teaspoon

OTHER

AC	alternating current
a.m./A.M.	hours from midnight to noon
amt.	amount
apt.	apartment
ave.	avenue
bldg.	building
blvd.	boulevard
Co.	company
c.o.d./C.O.D.	cash on delivery
da/d	day
DC	direct current
dept.	department
Dr.	doctor
ea.	each
etc.	and others
ex.	example
govt.	government
hosp.	hospital
hr/h	hour
info.	information
Jr.	Junior
M.D.	Doctor of Medicine
med.	medium
mgr.	manager
min.	minute
misc.	miscellaneous
mo.	month
mph	miles per hour
no.	number
p./pg.	page
pd.	paid
pkg.	package
p.m./P.M.	hours from noon to midnight
pymt.	payment
rd./Rd.	road
sq.	square
Sr.	Senior
st./St.	street
tel.	telephone
wk/w	week
wt.	weight
yr.	year

Blackline Master 7: World Map

Reading for Today

Certificate of Completion

This is to certify that

_____

has successfully completed *Level* ____
of Steck-Vaughn *Reading for Today* and has gained
the skill proficiency necessary to progress into *Level* ____ .

_____
Trainer

_____
Organization or Program

_____
City and State

_____
Date

STECK-VAUGHN
ELEMENTARY · SECONDARY · ADULT · LIBRARY

A Harcourt Company

Learner Placement Form

Read these words to your teacher.

Book 1	Book 2	Book 3	Book 4	Book 5
1. am	1. ran	1. take	1. try	1. plain
2. boss	2. tickets	2. mine	2. think	2. call
3. buy	3. send	3. hope	3. club	3. price
4. the	4. went	4. need	4. taught	4. show
5. car	5. ending	5. fight	5. sweet	5. died
6. from	6. rented	6. tune	6. clean	6. ground
7. go	7. mad	7. came	7. thank	7. mark
8. help	8. bet	8. sold	8. trip	8. town
9. I	9. I'm	9. seat	9. clock	9. draw
10. look	10. can't	10. worker	10. state	10. spoil
11. not	11. top	11. outlet	11. sleep	11. credit
12. run	12. red	12. who	12. shack	12. true
13. seven	13. we'll	13. women	13. skin	13. few
14. stop	14. cut	14. using	14. remind	14. worn
15. people	15. hand	15. truck	15. string	15. interest
16. us	16. win	16. many	16. roommate	16. smallest
17. to	17. hot	17. video	17. babies	17. worried
18. walk	18. she's	18. learn	18. clear	18. wouldn't
19. you	19. stopped	19. doctor	19. Saturday	19. myself
20. they	20. sitting	20. different	20. neatness	20. American

To the Instructor: Read the directions to the student. Allow 10 seconds for the student to read a word. Place the student in the *Reading for Today* book at which 3 of 5 consecutive words are first missed. If the student can read few or no words, place the student in the *Reading for Today Introductory Book.*